STEWARDSHIP

STEWARDSHIP

The Biblical Basis for Living

BEN GILL

foreword by
Dr. Robert H. Schuller

THE SUMMIT PUBLISHING GROUP

The Summit Publishing Group
One Arlington Centre
1112 East Copeland Road, Fifth Floor
Arlington, Texas 76011

Stewardship: The Biblical Basis for Living

Printed in the United States of America.
00 99 98 97 96 010 5 4 3 2 1

Library of Congress Cataloging-in-Publication Data
Gill, Ben, 1939 -
      Stewardship : the biblical basis for living / by Ben Gill.
            p. cm.
            Includes bibliogragphical references.
      ISBN 1-56530-208-7
            1. Stewardship, Christian, I. Title.
BV772.G54 1996
248'.6—dc20   96-10116
                                               CIP

Unless otherwise noted, quotations of Scripture are from the New King James Version, copyright 1979 by Thomas Nelson, Inc.

Cover and book design by David Sims

*This book is dedicated to all who will study and learn from it.
May the message of stewardship issue forth from your very soul
as you come to know the biblical basis for living.*

Contents

Foreword

God gives to humanity the privilege to be trustees of God's work, stewards of God's creation, and tenants of God's household. The dignity implied in this and the fulfillment found in this ennoble all of life. The businessman at his desk, the nurse at her station, the assembly-line worker, the mother with little children, and the elderly retiree all become co-workers with God when life is lived as stewards.

Years have passed since a comprehensive, biblical theological volume aimed at a widespread readership has been published and set forth for American church leaders and informed laypersons. The need for such a volume has grown by the year. With the aging of the donor base for our churches and institutions, we are facing a crisis of unthinkable proportions. The hour clamors for a volume of biblical teaching combined with practical application.

The name Ben Gill and the community of concern called Resource Services, Inc. are identified internationally with stewardship education and consultation. Over decades the integrity, professionalism, prayerfulness, reverence, and the stewardship of this group of stewards have become bywords to churches and institutions of all confessions.

It is my privilege to know Ben Gill, to take the measure of the man, to walk with him in the bonds of service. This book is a towering achievement by a man whose name and identity are synonymous with the highest and the best in Christian stewardship.

The bookshelves are barren of recent comprehensive works which combine biblical theology with an insight into the practical contemporary practice of stewardship. There are theological tomes that lack the practical. There are "how-to-do-it" books that are absent of the theological. There are books on specialized subjects—stewardship of the environment, etc.—that do not place these contemporary concerns in the context of the larger biblical revelation.

Ben Gill has offered the world a book that balances all of the above. There is the patient, exegetical work of a biblical scholar. There is the insightful, practical application of one who loves the church and knows the church's needs. There is the examination of cutting issues on the edge of contemporary stewardship. It is rare to find a book that moves from the exegesis of Greek texts to the discussion of contemporary genetic research. This book shows a Renaissance combination of scholarship, awareness of current issues, and practical guidance.

The hour cries for a new volume on stewardship. Never has the need been greater, the challenge more urgent, or the resources more necessary. Seventy thousand more people every day name Jesus Christ as Lord of life. The church explodes in Third World nations. North America thirsts for spiritual values. Single adults and families struggle with economic questions.

The consumerism of the 1980s has been replaced with a genuine struggle for values in the 1990s. Even secularists realize that a narcissistic lifestyle grants no ultimate fulfillment. One young man reaching a six-figure salary complained, "If this is all there is, what is it about?" People want to know how to be stewards.

It is a debate as old as Tolstoy whether the times produce the man or the man produces the times. Certainly, Ben Gill is a man for this time in the critical arena of stewardship. The arena is an appropriate metaphor. This book is not penned by an ivory-towered recluse. For three decades, Ben Gill has been in the arena where stewardship actually happens. He has seen firsthand the Spirit of God explode in some of the world's greatest and largest congregations with an outpouring of new stewardship. He has witnessed the heartache of misplaced stewardship and the victory of renewed stewardship. He is the incarnation of modern biblical stewardship.

This book belongs in every theological library, seminary, college, and university, and on the shelf of every pastor. The informed layperson and congregational leader should have it at hand.

As one who has seen God act through and on Christian stewards the world over, I commend this volume to the reading public.
—Robert Schuller

Acknowledgements

One is seldom wise in cataloging a list of contributors for fear of missing some vital link in the chain of life's development. But certain ones are so vividly with me on a daily basis that to fail in mentioning them would be a dastardly oversight.

My first exposure to biblical languages came in the classroom of Dr. William Tolar at Southwestern Theological Seminary. I suffered through "baby" Greek with hundreds of others, but this master of the Word imparted to me a love for the nuances of the language that continues to this day.

Dr. William Hendricks and Dr. John Newport, also at Southwestern Seminary, challenged my mind and demanded an educational base of cognitive thinking rather than rote memorization. They gave me the freedom to think and I am eternally in their debt for doing so.

At a point in my life when the burdens of life were great and the temptation to stop the walk was enticing, my friend, Dr. Edwin Young, senior pastor of the great Second Baptist Church in Houston, put his arm around me and said, "Ben, I am going to be praying for you." It was a simple gesture long forgotten by him, but I mention it here as a tribute for all the unnamed others who over the years have lifted me up as well. The road has never been too rough nor the mountains too steep simply because I was not on that road alone.

In my previous book, *The Joy of Giving*, I mentioned my ministry partner at RSI (Resource Services, Inc.), Bill Wilson. Bill and I have been serving together since college. Since the beginning of our work together we have worked with thousands of churches and raised billions of dollars for God's work. And throughout those years Bill has always been the one to see that we held to programming based on stewardship education. He has never been willing to go for the quick fix. His motto has always been, "Let's stand on the Word." I am a better person today because of his friendship.

The first time I ever experienced sound biblical exegesis was at the feet of Dr. W. A. Criswell, Pastor Emeritus of the First Baptist Church, Dallas, Texas. From the first moment I heard him expound on Isaiah I knew that I would not be satisfied in the shallows, but must learn to walk in the depths of the Word. And what an encourager he has been over the years. I am deeply indebted.

At my company, we have more than one hundred people who spend every day working with churches in programs of Christian stewardship. They are good people, dedicated to the cause and committed to the ministry. Over the years of our work together we have seen God work some great miracles among His people. We have all rejoiced together that we have been allowed to be a part of what God is doing. Because of their faithfulness, I have time to write books and make speeches and do other things that don't directly benefit them. I appreciate their willingness to allow me to be a part of their lives. Our work together brings joy to mine.

Finally, there is one other person who should be—must be—mentioned. Almost a year ago when I made the commitment to produce a textbook on Christian stewardship, I was wise enough to realize that I could not do the work alone. Therefore, I sought out one of the great theological minds of our day and requested his help in putting the pen to these thoughts and ideas. He graciously accepted on the condition that his work on this project be supportive in nature and always cloaked in the mantle of anonymity. I will respect that request while at the same time acknowledging that his contribution to the work is great and his influence through this volume eternal. I am deeply indebted to this modest pilgrim with whom for a time I have shared the journey.

Preface

In 1992, the research staff at our firm undertook a study of giving patterns in the Christian churches of our day. Extensive data was gathered and analyzed as we sought to determine the current status of financial stewardship in America. The results were both surprising and disturbing. In a nutshell, the church of the future is facing a funding disaster of onerous proportions as year by year the current donor base ages.

Upon reading the data I began to ask "Why?" Why, in a country as blessed by God as the America of the twentieth century, would the church of today or tomorrow face a funding disaster? In the search to answer that question, I went into the marketplace to find answers to this dilemma. Among laypeople there seemed to be a protectiveness in the process of stewardship. The common comment was something like this: "My church is always after money. Why can't they just let me give when I feel like it rather than always trying to make me feel guilty?"

Among the clergy the explanations were no less disturbing. One nationally known pulpiteer said to me, "I pride myself on the fact that in my twenty-eight years of ministry I have never once had to preach a sermon on stewardship."

I was astounded when I heard a seminary president say, "We teach no courses related to stewardship. We simply feel that there is no relevancy to that subject in the world of today."

After hearing countless others make similar statements I was struck with a shocking revelation: The problem facing our churches related to stewardship is not a funding problem; the problem is an educational problem. Over the years we have raised up laypeople, clergy, and educators who have no understanding of the biblical basis for stewardship. They believe stewardship is about money. They do not understand that it is about life. The answer to the problem of tomorrow is not going to be found in another slick program for the annual stewardship drive or some guilt-laden sermon for commitment Sunday. The answer is going to lie in a grounding in the Word as it relates to our purpose as God's creation.

During the course of this research I had an opportunity to visit with Dr. Maxie Dunnam, who was then senior minister of Christ Church in Memphis, Tennessee. He is currently president of Asbury Seminary. I expressed my dismay to Dr. Dunnam, who explained it is difficult to teach in this area since it lacks a significant work from which to teach. Knowing of my commitment to the ministry of Christian stewardship, Dr. Dunnam challenged me to produce such a manuscript. I departed his office with a commitment to delve into the Word and seek a deeper understanding of this tenet of the faith.

Such a pilgrimage is never taken alone. While I desperately wanted to hear the sonorous voice of God or experience my own burning bush—as a guide into the depths of Christian dogma—the experience did not come. What did come were hours of study, moments of despair, flights into ecstasy, and challenges to my long-held beliefs. And all along the path there were those whose contributions to my experiences brought color and vitality to the struggle.

It is proverbial that no book can do everything. Certainly, a subject as broad as stewardship could not be treated in an encyclopedia of volumes. I offer this work as a combination of the biblical, theological, and practical. Whereas the book cannot say everything about any one of these concerns, it touches on the roots and the matrix of each of them. I attempt to describe the basis of stewardship in the Bible, the Old and New Testament principles of stewardship, and the implication of stewardship for important areas of systematic theology.

The chapter on contemporary concerns touches on only a few of the hundreds of cutting-edge questions in stewardship. It is hoped that these few concerns will model an approach to the many.

Certainly, other passages could have been treated, other topics addressed, and other concerns expressed. I have attempted to put the heart of my concern about the biblical and the practical in this book. I trust the reader to enlarge on that under the Spirit's guidance.

What People Are Saying about *Stewardship*

"A biblically informed and comprehensive treatment of Christian stewardship that will meet the needs of many a pastor and all theological students."

Dr. Thomas Gillespie, President
Princeton Theological Seminary
Princeton, New Jersey

"Resource Services, Inc. was a valuable part of the stewardship ministry of Second Baptist Church as we sought to secure gifts for our church building program. The campaign that they led was not based only on the giving of dollars, but focused on a deeper level of giving all that we have and all that we are to our Lord, Jesus Christ. The spiritual impact remains with us to this day."

Dr. Ed Young, Senior Minister
Second Baptist Church
Houston, Texas

"A comprehensive treatment of stewardship from a biblical perspective has been needed for a long time. The theological and biblical undergirding needed for training God's people in the crucial area of stewardship is here. I highly recommend it."

> Dr. Frank Barker, Senior Minister
> Briarwood Presbyterian Church
> Birmingham, Alabama

"Ben Gill's thoughtful and clear presentation of Christian stewardship releases Christian leaders and laypeople from the shackles of guilt giving by reminding us that no human gift establishes our covenant with God—biblical giving is an act of gratitude honoring and reflecting God's unconditional love."

> Dr. Bryan Chapell, President
> Covenant Theological Seminary
> St. Louis, Missouri

"Ben Gill is a phenomenally gifted leader and has a lifelong dedication to and passion for Christian stewardship. I heartily recommend his new book."

> Bishop Claude E. Payne
> Episcopal Diocese of Texas
> Houston, Texas

"I am grateful that, at last, there is a biblical and balanced treatment of Christian giving in Ben Gill's new book, *Stewardship: The Biblical Basis for Living*. The message is rock-solid and powerfully instructive, both to the theological student and the church practitioner. All church leaders should digest this book and apply its principles to their own lives and then to their congregations."

> Dr. Jack Graham, Pastor
> Prestonwood Baptist Church
> Dallas, Texas

"Stewardship isn't just an issue for "practical" decision making. It is a topic of profound theological significance. We need an understanding of stewardship that is grounded in a careful study of God's gracious dealings with the creation. Ben Gill has provided us with such a study."

Dr. Richard J. Mouw, President
Fuller Theological Seminary
Pasadena, California

"The Church would do well to listen attentively to Ben Gill's contribution to stewardship education. Especially compelling, in light of an overly moralistic approach to such matters in the evangelical church today, is his emphasis on giving as a response to the gift of God's grace in the gospel of Jesus Christ."

Dr. Skip Ryan, Senior Minister
Park Cities Presbyterian Church
Dallas, Texas

"One of the greatest needs in the local church is to teach God's people God's plan of joyous giving. I heartily commend this text to prepare tomorrow's leaders to lead the people of God in the liberating power of biblical giving."

Dr. Jim Henry, Pastor
First Baptist Church
Orlando, Florida
President, Southern Baptist Convention

"I am so delighted to have Ben Gill's contribution to the ministry of stewardship. His book, *Stewardship: The Biblical Basis for Living,* will be a great help to pastors in local churches, as well as others who are interested in stewardship. Ben Gill has proved his commitment and his understanding of stewardship in his ministry across the nation. I don't know anyone who is more committed, and who knows more about Christian stewardship than Ben Gill."

Dr. Maxie Dunnam, President
Asbury Theological Seminary
Wilmore, Kentucky

"Seminarians need to be unswervably convicted regarding Christian stewardship. The local church will reflect that pastoral conviction. Ben Gill has made a significant contribution with his book, and I trust it will be widely used!"

Dr. Landrum P. Leavell, President
New Orleans Baptist Theological Seminary
New Orleans, Louisiana

"Is stewardship more than money? Is it biblical? Does it drive naturally from an appropriate theology and exegesis of biblical passages? Ben Gill has demonstrated in his book, *Stewardship: The Biblical Basis for Living*, that the answer to all of those questions is a resounding yes. But what is most amazing about this book is that it is, as far as I know, the first thoroughgoing theology of stewardship that understands the topic to embrace a great deal more than monetary means. Churches and seminaries need this volume."

Dr. Paige Patterson, President
Southeastern Baptist Theological Seminary
Wake Forest, North Carolina

"The American churches are now facing a crisis of stewardship. This has been a neglected theme and truth in pulpits of all denominations. Our materialistic society has spawned materialistic churches. We should welcome a serious biblical recovery of this urgent responsibility—Christian stewardship."

Dr. R. Albert Mohler, President
Southern Baptist Theological Seminary
Louisville, Kentucky

"It has been said that stewardship is the way that men make money and God makes men. I am grateful for *Stewardship: The Biblical Basis for Living*, and trust that it will have wide distribution."

Dr. Adrian Rogers, Pastor
Bellevue Baptist Church
Cordova, Tennessee

"Ben Gill knows more about stewardship in the church than anyone I know. Every Methodist should read this book."

Dr. Kenneth Wayne Day, Pastor
First United Methodist Church
Fort Worth, Texas

"This book reflects the same wisdom, practical understanding, and deep faith that has been such a gift to so many churches in Ben Gill's consulting ministry. Now he offers this wonderful contribution to the larger church—a theologically sound, eminently usable guide to the essential Christian ministry of stewardship development. It is a great gift to us all."

The Rev. Samuel T. Lloyd, III, Rector
Trinity Church, Copley Square
Boston, Massachusetts

"From the beginning of time to the end of the age, our stewardship of the manifold gifts and mysteries of God is our richest possession and our most glorious blessing. It is a vital part of the life of the church, of the life of the people of God, of the ministry of the pastor, and of the faithful servant of Christ wherever he stands and services in the kingdom of God.

To help us glorify the Lord in this stewardship assignment is the helpful and inspired work of Resource Services, Inc., whose chief executive officer is Ben G. Gill. Invite him and his distinguished fellow workers to work with you in the church, in the institution, and in the far-flung saving love and grace of our Lord Jesus Christ. Read this magnificent book and you will be glad that you did. You will be greatly enriched as you respond to the written challenge presented on these splendid pages."

Dr. W. A. Criswell, Pastor Emeritus
First Baptist Church
Dallas, Texas

"I know Ben Gill. His experience and integrity qualify him to author this reflective work. He suggests that our comprehension of biblical stewardship mirrors our most important attitudes and values. Jesus knew this. He spoke of money and other possessions and their symbolism more often than most other topics.

Americans are the world's greatest collectors of things. Our temporal piles of materials and emotionally dependent 'junk' blind us to the liberating truth of Christian living only available by distribution and management of our things. Gill says we can invest in eternity and begin to unload!"

Dr. Del Tarr, President
Assemblies of God
Theological Seminary
Springfield, Missouri

The Basis of Stewardship

T he very possibility of "steward-
ship" roots in biblical theism. The order of the adjective "biblical" and noun "theism" places the emphasis where it must rest.
God exists and speaks. The Bible as Word of God both contains
and is that divine self-disclosure. Apart from biblical theism, the
idea of humankind as steward finds little sustainable basis.

INADEQUATE WORLDVIEWS FOR STEWARDSHIP

Atheism, as a framework for life, has no rational basis for life as
stewardship. The naturalism demanded by atheism provides no
context for the physical or the temporal to belong to any entity, personal or corporate. In the atheistic framework everything
belongs to itself. There is no one to own anything and everything; there is nothing other than a social compact to ensure
private ownership of simple real property. The reductionism
that defines atheistic naturalism sees matter—both animate
and inanimate—as a fortuitous, random collection of atoms
permitted by the equally random laws of an uncreated and
untended universe.

It should be no historical surprise that atheism was the philosophical or ontological servant of communism. The idealistic absence of personal property in communist dogma must be served by the absence of the primal owner. If there is no ownership by God, there is no subsidiary ownership by human beings. The communist state became god/owner, thus the comrade became the steward of a subdivision of state property, only in connection with other comrades. There could be no sense of individual stewardship or ownership. Indeed, individual ownership was the communist political equivalent of the devil.

One can argue that the self-acknowledged failure of communism in the former Soviet Union is an admission that life cannot function in the absence of stewardship that is grounded in the sense of divine mandate.

Neither does stewardship find a place in the polar opposite of atheism—polytheism. A universe ruled by multiple gods creates a schizophrenia of multiple domains. The animist placates the tree spirit, the rock spirit, and the river spirit in a fractionalized "creation" that produces lifelong angst. The rococo Hindu temple carvings (with their crowded, frenzied display of multiple deities) reflect a faith without stewardship. The inertia created by the law of karma paralyzes any active sense of participation with a creating and owning God to whom in this one life the individual owes stewardship. Polytheism in its many expressions does not create the sense of steward in humankind.

Pantheism cannot sustain a consistent view of life as stewardship. For the pantheist there is no over-againstness with natural creation. When God is everywhere, God is actually nowhere in terms of personal accountability to God for one's stewardship of life. That God is nature (or conversely that nature is God) leaves no I-Thou relationship to empower accountability as a steward. It is one thing to experience a personal responsibility before Almighty God, maker of heaven and Earth, and quite another to conjure up an impersonal responsibility to a mountain stream.

A few modern expressions of environmental concern have bordered on pantheism. Granted the urgent need for stewardship of the environment, the ecosystem itself cannot extract from humans the accountability for sustaining that system. Nature cannot rise above itself. Unless there is a wholly and holy other who created and sustains nature and to whom I owe a personal trusteeship for the use of that nature, there can be no sustained concern for the environment.

Nor can an impersonal deism undergird a lifestyle of stewardship. The traditional deistic view that God "wound up the clock" and walked away to leave it running itself cannot enable stewardship as a way of life. An impersonal clockwork deity creating and then abandoning an equally impersonal universe induces no sense of personal responsibility for the creation.

Therefore, it is only in the immediacy of a personal theism that the groundwork for stewardship remains unshaken. But a personal (mono) theism must be further defined for an adequate view of stewardship. Islam projects a personal theism of sorts. Allah is One God, but not the God and Father of our Lord Jesus Christ. The absolute determinism of Islamic theism precludes a thoroughgoing stewardship. When the absolute will of Allah has already predetermined every condition of life, there is no dynamic interaction with a God who requires human response from trustees accountable to God for what they did with God's creation. One only need look at the Islamic world to see the

3

inertia created by a fatalistic determinism. Similarly, there is no need to save a rain forest if it has already been decreed by an inscrutable divine determinism that all will be incinerated. Fatalistic, deterministic theism that robs humankind of all initiative cannot produce a sense of stewardship.

Only a biblical theism provides the adequate theological context for a doctrine and practice of personal stewardship. Thus, stewardship belongs to the category of revealed religion. An adequate understanding of stewardship rests upon the principle that God is self-disclosed in the Word and without that disclosure there could be no comprehension of life as a steward. In that sense, there is no "natural" stewardship as an all-embracing conception of life. A natural philosophy of stewardship would always be tinctured by the heart of the human as *incurvatus en se*, turned in upon itself. A natural philosophy of stewardship would only choose self-serving domains or arenas of stewardship and neglect those less appealing. For example, the weekend off-roader might find stewardship of wilderness areas a personal interest, but not the stewardship of income for the work of God's Kingdom. Anything less than a revealed responsibility of stewardship fractionalizes stewardship on the basis of self-interest.

As the theological, indeed rational, basis for biblical stewardship rests on the creating activity of God, the biblical announcement of creation as a fact and God as the Creator precedes and justifies the concept of steward. The sonorous announcement "In the beginning Elohim created the heavens and the Earth" asserts the unchallenged priority of God as Creator/owner. One of the oldest biblical names for God, El, recalls one who is both strong and foremost. As a corollary, this postures humankind as finite, dependent, and limited. The plural form, Elohim, connotes by its plurality the majesty of the One thus introduced, the One who in the highest degree deserves awe.

With the coming of the Enlightenment, the biblical view of a creating God became the object of incessant opposition by rationalism, naturalism, and empiricism. The church retreated into either a concession or an accommodation to the spirit of the times. From the nineteenth century forward the emphasis on theology came to rest on the anthropocentric, the existential circumstance of man as man, of humankind as such. Thus, the center of gravity moved from the mighty creating act of God to the centrality of humans and their own dilemma. Such a shift from the center yielded inevitably a demotion of the doctrine of stewardship. There is a corresponding loss of emphasis on the central significance of God as Creator and humans as stewards when the creating act of God is shoved into the wings and the center of theology becomes an obsession with the human.

It is indeed an irony that at the very height of the technological achievement resting on the empiricism born out of the Enlightenment, the astronauts on the way to the moon read from the first chapter of the Bible the creating act of God. There they were atop the very epitome of scientific/technological achievement affirming that God is Creator and we are but stewards. Very few humans considered their reading inappropriate or a contradiction of what they were doing.

Not only is the divine creation by fiat, but the very literary expression of creation reflects the same peremptory economy of language. There are only two direct theological statements of the creation story in the Old Testament, the great statement of Elohim as Creator (Gen. 1:1 - 2:4a) and the simpler statement of Yahweh's activity in creation (Gen. 2:4b–25). The chief work of creation is that of humankind; the rest of the world is ordered around the creation of man and woman as the center of gravity in creation.

The absolute authority of God in the creative act resounds from the opening words of the biblical canon: "In the beginning God created the heavens and the Earth." Although there have long been questions about the best way to translate this sentence, it is clear that it is not to be read as a relative statement of time which permits any autonomy outside of God. As Walter Eichrodt said, "The narrator is moved to reflection not by that which preceded the divine creation but by the fact that nothing but the autonomous decree of the transcendent God determined the form of creation."[1]

This trenchant observation by Eichrodt underscores the nature of the creative act from the opening words of the biblical narrative. Creation is the self-determined announcement of God, contingent on absolutely nothing else in heaven and Earth. This earliest note already lays out the paradigm of God as owner and humans as stewards of that which God decreed.

The activity of that mighty One is *bārā'*, to form and to fashion that which has been cut out. Whether in the realm of physical creation or spiritual, *bārā'* refers to the act of God alone. The Hebrew verb was a technical term in the theological language of the priests and always refers to a divine creative act with no human analogy. It is always used as a verb and never has any subject but God. Nowhere is *bārā'* used of human production nor does it take as its object any form of matter. Thus, it implies the famed *creatio ex nihilo*, creation of something utterly new out of nothing. Although this theoretical construct cannot be based

on the verb *bārā'* alone, it is the implication. The first explicit
mention of *creatio ex nihilo* is reflected in the apocryphal 2 Macc.
7:28, a product of intertestamental theological reflection. Thus,
God becomes the primal owner of all the universe. There is no
preexistent stuff from which God fabricates creation. God calls
the very stuff of creation into existence by God's powerful Word.
God is the primal owner in a sense that humans can never be
owner. God does not own as the result of acquiring preexistent
matter. God owns by the right of calling matter out of nothing
into something. This places the divine right of ownership
beyond all question. If there were indeed some primeval matter
which stood against God in its eternity, God's unique ownership
might be called into question. As a result of God's originative
power, God created something fundamentally new, altogether
transcending the power of humans.

The significance of this prior ownership underpins any concept of human stewardship. The reverse of this can be seen in
sectarian movements of Hinduism which hold that matter is
eternal, a not uncommon view of some Eastern religions. It is of
no great surprise that such religious views do not promote a comprehensive view of stewardship. The passive view of life and time
reflects a deeply embedded philosophy of matter over or against
humanity. When inorganic matter preexists humans eternally,
the nerve of stewardship is severed and the concept of divine
ownership is nonexistent. The prevalent late–twentieth–century
secular concern with stewardship of the environment grew out of
the Judeo-Christian Western tradition, not the traditions of
Eastern religions which hold the eternal nature of matter over or
against God. Although humbly respectful in the face of the world
religious plurality, the Christian must insist that even secular

impulses toward preservation of environment have their roots in the biblical tradition. Western civilization now labors under a collective amnesia in that regard. As Elton Trueblood coined the phrase, we are a cut-flower civilization. We still produce the fruits of biblical stewardship, even though long since cut off from the roots. The conscious effort in the West to save endangered species, retain the rain forests, and to preserve the ozone express-es an impulse rooted in biblical stewardship. That heritage ener-gizes Western civilization with such vitality that even the "post-Christian" era resonates with the historic Christian con-sciousness of the Christian as steward.

Christians should not, however, expect that environmental preservation impulse to continue in the absence of a conscious biblical stewardship. As a current celebrated cause with the aura of appropriate ecological concern, the stewardship of the planet enjoys a temporary social approbation. Given the nature of human selfishness, such causes run their course and more immediate gratifications surface. Without the impetus provided by a rigorous biblical stewardship, the current environmental concern will find its days numbered.

The mysterious majesty of God in the creative act is further underscored by the divine Word in creation. God effects cre-ation by simply uttering a word. This implies the effortlessness of God's creative activity. Only the verbal assertion of the divine will calls matter and order out of a void and chaos. The creation by the sheer expression of will further reflects the lord-ly ownership of God. As Gerhard von Rad states, "If the world was called into being by the free will of God, then it is his very own possession, and he is its Lord."[2]

Behind this rests the image of the absolute word of the oriental potentate in his court. That courtiers, vice-regents, or satraps acted immediately and without question to the lordly word underscored the absolute ownership of all people and things by the enthroned potentate. Creation by word alone easily suggested ownership to the first readers of the text. It only recalled to them the model of the political structure in which they lived: A king who owned everything and everybody.

The creative act of Elohim takes place within time. "Creation is regarded as a work of Yahweh in history, a work within time. This means there is a real and true opening up of historical prospect."[3] Thus, the earliest narratives lay a foundation for seriously considering time as a stewardship of life. Had creation been an act outside the historic continuum, time itself would have been an afterthought subsidiary to the creative process. In other words, if all clocks suddenly stopped at once and humans lived in a world without the record of time, the seriousness of each hour would evaporate. That God created within time rather than before time sanctifies all time. The eternal has entered the temporal and by that entering has made the temporal holy and accountable. Thus, Paul could make his noted appeal that humans be about "redeeming the time, because the days are evil" (Eph. 5:16). The implication of this Pauline mandate casts its shadow all the way back inside the gates of Eden. God created in time with an intention for time. That time is capable of redemption implies that time itself has fallen but can be restored. In the beginning, God hallowed time as part of human stewardship. Redeemed humanity must participate in buying back that time as part of stewardship. The one self-identified as "I AM THAT I AM" has entered into that succession of intervals we call time. Forever after time must be taken seriously as a stewardship of value. Luke takes great pains at the beginning of Jesus' public ministry to place it in the great Lucan synchronic naming imperial and Hebrew religious and political figures of the time (Luke 3:1-3). Just as creation took place within time and sanctifies time, so also the mighty acts of redemption take place within real time and sanctify that time. Indeed, Western civilization primarily remembers the Augustan and Tiberian eras because they bracketed the ministry of the Lord Jesus.

The Christian faith always hallows time. It renders to time that sense of urgency that belongs to time as *kairos* rather than *kronos*. Time is not merely a succession of chronological moments. Time is kairotic time, time pregnant with significance and fraught with destiny. This often-noted linear view of time stands out as the biblical contribution to temporal value. In contrast, Baalism reflected that cyclical view of time which has no omega point, no denouement. Baalism embraced a view of time that envisioned life as an endlessly repeated cycle mirrored in the agricultural seasons of Palestine. Baalism was a treadmill of existence illustrated by the yoked animal treading out the grain of the harvest in meaningless circles of repetition. Biblical faith sees time as moving from the mighty act of God to the next mighty act of God. Once again, Western civilization has forgotten its serious view of time. The crowded rush of urban streets and the mania of time efficiency that fills out Daytimers are not just reminders of American efficiency. Behind the American view of time as value rests the biblical view of time as significant. We are stewards who cannot remember the reason for our stewardship: In time God created as the owner of time.

The Old Testament places the most intimate sense of createdness in humans' reflections upon themselves. The people of the Old Testament quickly moved from the fact of God as the Creator in the beginning to the reality of God as the Creator of every human life. God "gives breath to the people on it [the Earth], and spirit to those who walk on it" (Isa. 42:5). Job acknowledges that God fashioned him in every detail (Job 10:8-12). Jeremiah (18:1-6) and Isaiah (64:8) compare God to a potter who sovereignly shapes the clay, humans. Psalm 139 is the mighty confession of one who understands himself totally in terms of God's creation. Yet this sense of createdness does not render humans as servile minions, cringing lackeys of a heavenly overlord. "Along with this sense of createdness goes the conviction of the God-given dignity of man and lordship over the rest of creation," wrote Robert Butterworth.[4]

The place of humankind in the scheme of creation demonstrates the relative immediacy of humans in relationship to the creating God. Whereas the watery chaos stands at the greatest distance from the creating God, humans stand at the apex of creation in the closest relationship to the Creator. In Genesis 1, humanity enters the stage on the sixth day, the long-awaited star of creation. All other creatures are simply introductory acts to the main attraction, the human race (Gen. 1:26-27). In Genesis 2, humans formed from the dust of the Earth are nevertheless God's primary concern. All other creation occupies the wings of the stage while human beings take center stage. Is this anthropocentric view of creation an arrogant narcissism in which bit players in an impersonal cosmos try to seize center stage? Is humanity actually the apex of creation? Freud, in *Moses and Monotheism* and *The Future of an Illusion*, stated just that. Wrestling with its own mortality, Freud's humanity created the infantile illusion that it stood at the center when in reality it is a preposterously marginal species. Humans projected a caring Father God to fill the eternal void of nothingness in an impersonal universe. Faith is nothing but a projection of human need. We are eternal infants at the center of our own world.

The biblical witness contradicts the rationalism of Freud's severe judgment. The Creator is the one decisive witness in favor of humankind's central position. The biblical history of Israel shows a failed chosen people marginalized in history by the superpowers who do not know Yahweh. In the biblical reflection on its own history, Israel painfully chronicled that it failed to be the center of its own Levantine world, no less the center of creation. The maintenance of the exalted view that humans are the center of creation was an act of absolute faith in the face of the failed mission of the creation. From outside the gates of Eden, Israel peered back inside and, against all rational observation of its own history, maintained that humans are more angel than ape. Christoph Barth summarizes this tension:

> Why is humanity granted this outstanding position? It is not because of any theory of human priority in natural history, nor because of optimistic views of humanity. It is because it is God's plan, purpose, and intention for humanity. It pleases God that humanity should be his partner in an adventure of voluntary obligation and relationship.[5]

Far from being mere anthropocentric narcissism, the Genesis story is thoroughly theocentric. It is not humankind's exalted view of itself but God's own view of the volitional act of creation that predominates. Remember that Genesis 1 is the prologue to the painfully honest story of the antediluvian humanity and the portraits of the patriarchs "warts and all."

The elevation of humans as the apex of creation flies in the face of all that follows. It is God who calls us to that grand destiny from above. Otherwise we would grovel in the dirt rather than exalt in the divinity of our origin.

The significance of this exalted origin cannot be overstated in considering stewardship. It would be absurd to consider the stewardship of my dog. That would be an outcome not equal to the origin of the dog. That the dog should be the steward of its house, yard, and bowl is ridiculous even to consider. The origin of the dog and the dog's absolute lack of self-consciousness as to any origin makes the very concept of stewardship a farce. It is in contrast to all other creation that humans both have and know that they have an exalted origin by the will of God. It is the self-conscious knowledge of that origin as crown of creation that empowers the view of life as stewardship.

In the Bible, human identity stands between God on the one side and the rest of creation on the other. Humans are not merged into God; they are separate creations. Yet humans are set apart from everything else that is created. Yet "the biblical way of defining human being is from first to last relational. We are who we are . . . in relationship to the others with whom we live, move, and have our being," wrote Douglas John Hall.[6]

In the biblical account, humans are not merely caught up in a mindless, mystic contemplation of God. Humans in their very existence want to know who they are in relationship to God and to the things around them, animate and inanimate. Stewardship, the relationship as a trustee with responsibility to all creation around humans, belongs to the presuppositions of biblical revelation. Creation is never considered as an objective thing in itself back toward which we look with awe but detachment. We are humans-in-relationship with the God of creation and everything else God created. This relatedness is at the very heart of biblical stewardship.

In the early church, the hermits and the "pillar saints" who sat atop pillars separated and isolated missed this point—as do all obsessive asceticism and mystic detachment. We are bound together with all creation, animate and inanimate.

Emil Brunner stated this tension in his great Christian anthropology, Man In Revolt. The ordinary man is aware of this tension within himself. He recognizes that there is a higher element, but he also knows there is a lower. Yet we cannot understand this tension of being part of creation and yet somehow above all other creation because we are tangled up in our own createdness. "To see truly we need to be at a distance, or at a certain elevation; if we were above the contradiction we would be both it and the source of the 'higher' element in man," Brunner stated.[7] To understand this tension that places us somewhere between ape and angel we must understand what it means to be created in the image of God.

All of this is preparatory to the concept of humans as created in the image of God, the imago dei. Gen. 1:26-27 introduces the creation of humankind with a special solemnity. It is introduced as the result of a special deliberation on the part of the heavenly council. The well-noted plural "let us create Adam ('man') in our image" reflects the deliberations of the heavenly council, the heavenly equivalent of the court of the Eastern potentate. Out of this fullness of deliberation, God creates. Singled out from all other creations, Adam is created in the image and the likeness of God. Both words should be taken as representing some aspect of God's spiritual nature as over or

against, one being material and the other being spiritual in con-
notation. Obviously, the image of God is that which sets
humankind apart from the rest of creation. It is something that
is passed on to descendants and belongs therefore to humankind
in general, not just to Adam and Eve in Eden. However mutat-
ed it might be, image is not effaced in the life of any human
beyond some faint reflection of Eden. Samuel R. Driver considers the imago from the standpoint of the older school of thought
that attributed it to the rational nature of humans:

> It can be nothing but the gift of self-conscious reason,
> which is possessed by man, but by no other animal. In all
> that is implied by this—in the various intellectual faculties
> possessed by him, in his creative and originative power
> enabling him to develop and make progress in arts, sci-
> ences, and in civilization generally; in the power of rising
> superior to the impulses of sense, of subduing and trans-
> forming them; of mounting to the apprehension of general
> principles, and of conceiving intellectual and moral ideals;
> in the ability to pass beyond ourselves and enter into rela-
> tions of love and sympathy with our fellowmen; in the pos-
> session of a moral sense, or the faculty of distinguishing
> right and wrong; in the capacity for knowing God and hold-
> ing spiritual communion with Him—man is distinguished
> fundamentally from other animals, and is allied to the
> Divine nature; so that, wide as is the interval separating
> him from the Creator, he may nevertheless, so far as his
> mental endowments are concerned, be said to be an
> "image," or adumbration, of Him.[8]

In the classical sense, Driver reflects that path originated by
Irenaeus and followed by Christian doctrine until the
Reformation. There is in Genesis 1 the double expression
"image" and "likeness":

> Hebrew ṣelem and dᵉmût
> Greek ikon and homoiosis
> Latin imago and similitudo

Whatever these two words mean, it rests at the heart of humankind's place in the world. The Catholic Church did and does distinguish between two elements in humans: the image of God consists in the freedom and rationality of human nature. The likeness of God is human self-determination under God, the gift of communion with God. In Catholic theology humans lost the second and kept the first. This classical "two story" view of humans is a dualism and does not allow humans the reality and dignity of being a unity. Luther with his inherent common sense of exegesis rejected this dualism. He saw humankind as a unity. What is left in humans is the relic of God's image in humankind. This marred relic has remained. It remained to Karl Barth to take this to an ultimate extreme; even the relic of the image has been destroyed. The fact that "man is man and not a cat" is "quite unimportant."[9]

What then does it mean to be created in the image of God, if it is not to be understood in these static images of classical theology? Brunner insists that we understand the image of God in terms of someone who is actively addressed by God and whose destiny is found in responding to that call as grace. In a beautifully memorable passage Brunner represents it this way:

> The being of man, in contrast to all other forms of creaturely being, is not something finished, but it is a being-in-self-knowledge and a being-in-self-determination. Figuratively speaking, God produces the other creatures in a finished state; they are what they ought to be, and this they remain. But God retains man within His workshop, within His hands. He does not simply make him and finish him; human nature, indeed, consists in the fact that we may and must remain in the hands of God. The creatures which have not been endowed with reason are turned out as finished articles. The characteristic imprint of man, however, only develops on the basis of the divine determination, as an answer to a call, by means of a

decision. The necessity for decision, an obligation which he can never evade, is the distinguishing feature of man.[10]

What then is the implication of this for humans as stewards? In the classical and Reformation views humans could be left with no real ability to recognize life in the world as a life of stewardship. If Brunner's reckoning of the biblical view is right, stewardship itself becomes part of that ongoing call of God. God is always calling out to us to be God's trustees, and we must always in grace be responding to that call. Stewardship is not one remote decision grounded in the past; the essence of life as a steward is a daily answering to the call of God. Stewardship is not the static signing of a pledge card in the annual drive (although this concreteness is not without significance). Stewardship is a responding with my "Yes" to God's constant call that I live life in God's image, as God's steward responding to God's will. This sense of being daily addressed as a steward uplifts life from the banal struggle for existence and places it on a plane of the redemptive.

This view of the image as revealed in human rationality belongs to the typical theology of the nineteenth century—a century imbued with the idea of endless progress and ascent of human achievement, it was easier to see human rationality as a reflection of God. The absurdities of the twentieth century have made this rationalistic optimism less palatable. The irrationalities of the Holocaust and the recent menace of mutually assured destruction have rendered the divine rationality of the human species less likely. Driver, and the traditional schools of thought on the image of God, missed the sense of a dynamic, ongoing, interactive relationship with God. The image is not a substance poured into Adam or a quantum of some spiritual stuff allocated to humans. The image must therefore exist in some kind of dynamic tension, an ongoing interface between the Creator and the created.

Further, creation is never considered as an end in itself. It is the first of the mighty acts of God that would result in the call of Abraham, the history of Israel, and ultimately the Redemption accomplished in Christ.

The Old Testament
Expression of Stewardship

In virtually the same divine breath that created humankind, the creating God commanded, "Let them have dominion over the fish of the sea, over the birds of the air, and over the cattle, over all the Earth and over every creeping thing that creeps on the Earth" (Gen. 1:26). These words encompass the great fourfold biblical division of the animal world: the aquatic, the avian, the domestic, and the wild animal kingdoms. Their sonorous repetition underscores the comprehensive nature of the world over which humans are to rule, or hold dominion. Indeed, the very image of God may be equated by the great Old Testament anthropologist Hans Walter Wolff as "the steward of the world."[1]

THE DOMINION OF HUMANKIND AS STEWARDSHIP IN THE WORLD

In the creation narrative God addresses Adam in a way unlike any other creation. God had addressed inanimate and animate creation with commands, but Adam is singled out as the object of God's continued address. That continued address is the very basis of dominion as stewardship. Psalm 8 expounds on the nature of this creation-for-dominion. The Psalm opens with an exclamation of the excellence found in God's name: "How excellent is Your name in all the Earth" (v. 1). But what constitutes that excellence?

> For You have made him a little
>   lower than the angels,
> And You have crowned him with glory and honor.
> You have made him to have
>   dominion over the works of
>   Your hands;
> You have put all things under
>   his feet,
> All sheep and oxen—
> Even the beasts of the field,
> The birds of the air,
> And the fish of the sea
> That pass through the paths of
>   the seas (Ps. 8:5-8).

Psalm 8 resonates as a theological commentary on the creation story. The very center of that story according to the psalmist is the dominion of humankind, the stewardship given to humans over natural creation. This dominion is so extensive that it extends even to the "paths of the seas." To the Hebrew mind this last expression only makes more marked the comprehensive nature of human stewardship through dominion. The sea was, for the Hebrew, an untamed threat. The Hebrews were not a sea-going people like their Phoenician neighbors. The sea represented the attempted reassertion of initial chaos overcome in the creative act of God. That humans have been given dominion even over the sea is an indication of the totality of their dominion. Our stewardship embraces all of God's creation.

In the expanded commentary of creation found in Gen. 2:15-25, humankind is given responsible tasks (2:15-17) and powers of decision (2:18-23). The responsibility of stewardship echoes immediately in the command to "tend" the garden, which means to cultivate the garden. Only God could create the garden, but humans must "tend" it. That is, even before the fall there was a stewardship that was given by God.

Wolff goes so far as to say that it is precisely in their function as rulers that humans are created in God's image.[2] Humans are to have a dominating relationship over creation. They are to subdue the Earth. Humankind's "crowning" in Psalm 8 is in "ruling" and in the fact that "all things are put under his feet."

This is made clearer by the ancient Eastern custom of setting up a ruler's statue as a proclamation of the ruler's dominion over the area where the statue was erected (cf. Dan. 3:1, 5-6). When in the thirteenth century BC the Pharaoh Ramses II had his statue cut out of the rock on the Mediterranean north of Beirut, the image meant that Ramses ruled that area. Wolff makes the striking statement:

> Accordingly man is set in the midst of creation as God's statue. He is evidence that God is the Lord of creation; but as God's steward he also exerts his rule, fulfilling his task not in arbitrary despotism but as a responsible agent. His rule and his duty to rule are not autonomous; they are copies.[3]

Humans stand in the world as the very image of God's rule in the world. The rulership of humans, however, is not an unregulated impulse to dominate. It is rather like the authority of a vice-regent or overseer who governs for another. Indeed, it is the very sense of stewardship that keeps humankind's rule in the world from being a despotic assertion of human power over all other creation. Humans are in authority, as Jesus would suggest much later, because humans are under authority. Even the relationship of man and woman in marriage is part of that dominion of stewardship. It is because the woman is a helpmate that together they are able to extend that dominion and the stewardship for the world. Through that union the multiplication of humans increases their dominion over the Earth. It was God's intention that a great mass of humanity with a multitude of members would rule over the Earth.

Clearly, the nature of human stewardship is absolute dominance. The Hebrew word *kibšuha* indicates the radical nature of human rule over the planet (Gen. 1:28). The radical *kbš* in Hebrew could point to the subjection of a country through war (Num. 32:22, 29), of slaves (Neh. 5:5), or even point to the rape of women (Esth. 7:8). The word always means the reduction of something to human use through the application of force (Josh. 18:1). Humans are given radical authority to dominate the world, but only as stewards, not as exploiters. That which keeps human force from running amuck is the nature of that force as stewardship. Humans are to oversee the planet for its creating Lord. It is only in the understanding of human dominion as stewardship that a hedge is built to protect creation from the perverted powers of humans. When life is not understood as stewardship, then humans use other humans as things and treat the environment as a thing to be exploited rather than a trust to be kept. The human thrust to domination is an awesome divine gift. Kept under the original stewardship command of God, it is the very image of God. Turned loose on the world without a sense of stewardship, it becomes the very image of perverted power—the temptation to turn stones to bread for the sake of one's own insatiable desire to dominate and to use for selfish ends.

THE WORLD AS THE OBJECT OF HUMAN STEWARDSHIP

The domain of human dominance, the arena of our stewardship, embraces the entire Earth. Animals in particular are named. For the ancient Old Testament world, the mastery of humankind over animals constituted a far greater marvel than merely making the earth yield food. And that mastery becomes even more significant as it tiers up from mere domestic animals to wild animals. When it moves to the hollow-boned birds that fly in the air it becomes for the Old Testament person even more mysterious. Most awesome of all is dominion over fish that swim invisibly in the trackless paths of the ever-threatening sea.

Ludwig Kohler captures the significance of this in a quotation as masterful in its grasp as it is poignant in its current application:

> This [Gen. 1:28] is the commission to establish civilization. It applies to all men and it embraces every age. There is no human activity that is not covered by it. The man who found himself with his family in an unprotected plain exposed to ice-cold wind and first laid a few stones one upon another and invented the wall, the basis of all architecture, was fulfilling this command. The woman who first pierced a hole in a hard thorn or a fishbone and threaded a piece of animal sinew through it in order to be able to join together a few shreds of skin, and so invented the needle, sewing, the beginning of all the art of clothing, was also fulfilling this command. Down to the present day, all the instructing of children, every kind of school, every script, every book, all our technology, research, science and teaching, with their methods and instruments and institutions, are nothing other than the fulfillment of this command. The whole of history, all human endeavor, comes under this sign, this biblical phrase.[4]

However effaced or defaced that image of God might be, all the activities of humankind that demonstrate the building of civilization reflect that original mandate. To see this most clearly, one must only contrast the achievements of the highest primate in comparison with those of humans. The gap between the most miserably ignorant, impoverished, and disabled human and the most highly trained primate cannot be bridged. That gap is a chasm that yawns. From the bottom of that chasm cries this ineffable difference: humans were created in the image of a Creator.

The fact that humans were created for dominance has important implications regarding our stewardship of all things which cannot be overstated. The only thing which can keep the human race from destroying its own habitat by mindless exploitation or by creating a self-destructing technological nightmare is the sense of stewardship concerning that over which we have been given dominance. Ultimately, it is only a sense of stewardship through Jesus Christ that can enable the human race to overcome its own will to power distorted from God's original intention.

THE PEOPLE OF GOD AS STEWARDS

The Old Testament backdrop of stewardship must be understood not only in terms of the creation account, but also as reflections of the principle terms of Old Testament community life: covenant, the promised land, worship, and mission.

Covenant as a Foundation of Stewardship

That covenant constitutes a primary motif of divine/human relations rests beyond question. The Hebrew word *berît* occurs no less than 278 times in the Old Testament. Further, the distribution of the word indicates its pervasive category in Hebrew thinking. *Berît* appears eighty times in the Pentateuch, ninety-seven times in the historical books, seventy-six times in the prophets, and twenty-five times in the poetic books.[5]

Although some instances of covenant refer to relationships among humans, the principle use in the Old Testament is in a religious sense. It is not too much to say that the concept of *berît* is the single most significant integrating factor in the Old Testament revelation. There are three primary understandings of covenant as it is used in the biblical framework. Some see the idea of covenant as one of mutuality. This places the emphasis upon a reciprocity that might imply an equality of the two parties involved. A second viewpoint sees *berît* as implying a relationship between two unequal partners. In this view the maker of a covenant is a power-figure who unilaterally makes a covenant with a relatively passive recipient of the covenant. A third viewpoint has gained momentum in recent decades. It interprets the Old Testament covenant against the backdrop of the so-called suzerainty treaty used in Western Asia in the second millennium BC. When a political overlord conquered a new area, he offered terms to a vassal state. The vassal could only receive the treaty as offered. Yet the treaty was not a bare power play. It opened by reminding the vassal of the acts of benevolence toward the vassal by the conquering party. The emphasis rests not on the mutual but on the unilateral character of the covenant.

Nowhere in scripture can one read of a covenant between God and a human in which it is said, "The two of them made a covenant." God only and always initiates the covenant. Humans respond to the covenant, but God initiates that covenant. In the first use of *berît* it is God who makes the covenant and calls it "My covenant" (Gen. 6:18). The same is true of God's covenant with Noah, Abraham, Israel at Sinai, and with David. God lays down the terms of the covenant; it is not negotiated. God expects a response from humans, but the covenant is not a covenant between equals.

The first mention of the word berît in the Bible indicates the stewardship-intense nature of covenant. When God made a covenant with Noah (Gen. 6:18), the latter understood that covenant in terms of an immediate stewardship of the Earth's animal life. The very same litany of domesticated animals, wild animals, and birds that was in the original command for dominion is repeated as the object of Noah's stewardship in the construction of the ark. The fish are obviously not named; supposedly they would survive the flood in their own habitat. Noah's existence was devoted to God's command that he act as a steward for the preservation of the animal life God had created. From the very first mention of the concept covenant in the Old Testament, the word is always connected with a stewardship of that which God has given.

Further covenants were solemnized by an act of sacrifice in the making of the covenant. The technical name for the execution of a covenant in the Old Testament was kārāt berît, which means "to cut" a covenant. The "cutting" might refer directly to the sacrifice by which the covenant was ratified. The covenant with Abraham, the prototype of the biblical covenant, was sanctified and solemnized in and by an act of stewardship. After the conditions of the covenant were announced to Abraham, Yahweh commanded Abraham to bring a heifer, a goat, a ram, a turtledove, and a pigeon. Abraham cut these sacrificial animals in two and placed the pieces in juxtaposition with one another (Gen. 15:10). At sundown a "deep sleep" (Heb. tardēmāh, the same sleep of Adam in Gen. 2:21) came on Abraham. In this dream theophany, a torch and a "smoking oven" pass between the pieces. The symbolism is that of God passing through the pieces of sacrificial animal. The sole focus is upon the activity of God in the covenant and the passive role of Abraham in receiving the covenant in grace, even as Abraham dreamed. He literally could not have been more passive. This underscores the unilateral nature of the covenant as the act of God.

In one regard Abraham was active in the covenant; he responded to the offer of the covenant with an act of sacrifice. The first and only immediate response was an offer of a stewardship gift to the God of the covenant. In the prototypical covenant, the appropriate response to God's covenant with humankind is the offering of a sacrifice, an acknowledgment of stewardship. This stewardship became the actual religious ceremony that sealed the covenant and constituted it as sacred. One cannot overlook the obvious relationship between God's covenant with Abraham and the offering of a gift to God. The latter flowed as naturally from the former as summer follows spring.

In that covenant, which constituted the theocracy of Israel at Sinai, the response of the congregation to the covenant was likewise the offering of sacrifice. Early in the morning, Moses built an altar at the foot of Sinai, surrounded by twelve pillars. The young men of the camp offered oxen on the altar (Exod. 24:4-5). Part of the blood was sprinkled on the people with the affirmation "This is the blood of the covenant which the Lord has made with you according to all these words" (v. 8). One can only wonder at the dramatic pathos of this scene. The awestruck Hebrews stood in reverence as the crimson splotches of animal blood were thrown toward them and stained their robes. It literally marked them as people of the covenant. Yet that covenant was once again ratified in an act of stewardship. The marking of the Hebrews not only reminded them of the covenant at Sinai, but also that the covenant was sealed with a sacrificial gift to the God whose thunderous presence shook the mountain. Once again the covenant-stewardship connection is unavoidable.

It becomes obvious that the first appropriate response of humans to God's covenant is an act of stewardship. It was unthinkable to biblical believers that any response could be made to the covenant other than that of a reverential offering of stewardship to God.

God's Ownership of the Covenant People

Flowing both into and out of the covenant motif is the fundamental assertion of God's ownership of the Hebrews. This ownership expressed itself in both God's choice of and redemption of God's people, i.e., in election and Exodus. In the pivotal events of Sinai following the Exodus, former slaves were claimed as God's own possession chosen from among all the peoples (Exod. 19:5). Ps. 33:12 asserts that the Hebrews are the "inheritance" of God and Ps. 135:4 that it was as a possession that God chose the Hebrews. The nature of God's ownership is clearly indicated by the use of *segullāh* to describe the Hebrews. The expression is used in this sense six times (Exod. 19:5; Deut. 7:6; 14:2; 26:18; Ps. 135:4; Mal. 3:17).

As used in Old Testament culture, the *segullāh* was that treasure which peculiarly and particularly belonged to the king. In the ancient mind, the king owned all things. Since the king owned all things, the joy of particular and discrete ownership evaded the king. Thus, the view developed that the king should have a peculiar personal treasure, a *segullāh*. This could be a

28

silken or leather pouch of gemstones or precious metals which the king might finger as a Greek would finger worry beads, to remind the king of his treasure. In this sense the word *segullāh* refers to Israel's relationship to God. From among all the peoples of the Earth owned by Yahweh, Israel is God's peculiar possession. Ownership is further indicated in the act of calling Israel "by name" (Isa. 43:1). For God to call the name of an individual or nation is an act of appropriation, choice, and ownership.

Equally profound as a basis for stewardship in the Old Testament is God's redemption of the Hebrews. Ps. 74:2 makes it clear that Yahweh redeemed Israel to be the people of God's inheritance. Isa. 43:1 might refer either to the redemption from Egypt or from Babylon. It specifically asserts "I have redeemed you...You are Mine." Another emphasis in Old Testament divine redemption is that of redemption by paying a price. The Old Testament emphasizes repeatedly that God redeemed Israel by the payment of a price (Exod. 15:13). This payment of price did not exclude the tender emphasis of personal divine oversight. God reminds the people of God's care: "I bore you on eagles' wings, and brought you to Myself" (Exod. 19:4). Stewardship in the Old Testament rests on God's ownership of the people of God, an ownership made double in the divine realities of election and redemption.

This ownership of God finds expression in numerous statements. Ps. 24:1 makes the inclusive statement: "The Earth is the Lord's, and all its fullness; the world and those who dwell therein." Israel is the firstborn son of Yahweh (Exod. 4:22). Yahweh is the Father of Israel (Jer. 31:9). Mal. 2:10a appeals to the fatherhood of God: "Have we not all one Father?" Yahweh appealed to Pharaoh, "Let My people go" (Exod. 5:1). Thus, the very basis of the Exodus was the ownership of God. "We are His people and the sheep of His pasture" (Ps. 100:3c). Such statements could be multiplied ad infinitum from biblical literature. Particularly significant for stewardship is the idea of Israel as God's "inheritance." Repeatedly, Israel is motivated to its destiny before God on the basis of being God's inheritance (Deut. 4:20; Deut. 9:29; 1 Sam. 10:1b; Jer. 12:7).

Much of Hebrew culture was dominated by the idea of inheritance. For the son to inherit the father's land indicated the son's possession of that land. The metaphor of inheritance is another way of stating God's ownership of the Hebrew people. Different as a metaphor, but implying the same ownership, is the emphasis on Israel as the "servant" of Yahweh (Isa. 41:8-16; 44:1-4; 48:20-21; Jer. 30:10). In a world where slaves were the absolute property of masters, the insinuation of servanthood for Israel only more strongly stated Yahweh's ownership of the people of God. Thus, by creation, covenant, election, redemption, and outright statement of ownership, Yahweh asserts a claim over the people as those responsible to be stewards. But this claim extends beyond the people. It also includes the land and the people's possessions.

The People of the Land

Inescapably tied to the nexus of stewardship and covenant is the land of Israel. Israel is the "Holy Land" not because the dirt is intrinsically holy, but because the people of Israel were to respond to the land in a certain way, a religio-ethical way that can only be called a stewardship of the land. Eliezer Schweid notes that the land of Israel can be conceptualized in seven ways from the Old Testament.[6]

- First, the borders of the land place it "in the middle." This "middleness" transcends the merely physical. The land does exist between the desert and the sea and between the great empires of Egypt and the Mesopotamia. But its placement "in the middle" is part of its stewardship in history. It makes Israel the arena in which God acts in the midst of the nations.
- The second viewpoint on the land embraces its natural characteristics. Israel is an abundant land that contains within its own borders all that is necessary to sustain a nation (Deut. 8:7-10). The covenant of God immediately ties Israel to the stewardship of this abundance.
- A third biblical perspective recalls the history of the land. Before Israel belonged to the Hebrews, it was considered the land of Canaan, land of the Amorites, and the land of the Hittites. The chief characteristic of these people was an idolatry that desacralized the land. The destiny of Israel was a stewardship of history in which the purposes of the land were reclaimed.
- A fourth biblical understanding of the land was that of promise. To the patriarchs, Moses, and repeatedly to the people (even after they were living in the land), the land was promised to the people on the condition of certain religio-ethical responses of the people. The people lived under a stewardship of this promise. They were the trustees in history of God's promises related to the land.
- A fifth motif of the land is that of conquest. The land was to be taken and the idolatrous relics of previous cultures were to be destroyed in the taking. One can rightly speak of a stewardship of conquest, a taking of the land as response of trusteeship given by God for the land.

- A sixth complex of views about the land focused on the way the people were to live in the land. It is in this realm that the stewardship of the land moves to the fore. The people of God were to live in the land as self-conscious stewards of the land. That stewardship was to be expressed in everyday life and in acts of worship symbolizing the stewardship. This relationship to the land is especially marked by the Sabbath of the seventh year:

> Six years you shall sow your field, and six years you shall prune your vineyard, and gather its fruit; but in the seventh year there shall be a sabbath of solemn rest for the land, a sabbath to the Lord. You shall neither sow your field nor prune your vineyard. What grows of its own accord of your harvest you shall not reap, nor gather the grapes of your untended vine, for it is a year of rest for the land. And the sabbath produce of the land shall be food for you. (Lev. 25:3-6; cf. Exod. 23:11; Deuteronomy 15).

This vision of a sabbath for the land provokes one to look at a spectrum of biblical concerns. At the center of these concerns is the stewardship of the land. As man rests one day in seven, the land rests one year in seven. At the end of a septenary series of seven years, at the fiftieth year there is to be a year of jubilee (Lev. 25:9) which involves an even more radical stewardship of the land and life. In this nexus covenant, land, and stewardship weave themselves together in a tapestry from which no thread can be pulled without ruining the pattern. This stewardship of the land works itself out practically in the portions of dough set aside for the priests, tithes and offerings of the firstfruits in the Temple, and crops that were to be left over in the field at harvest time to be collected by the poor (Lev. 22, 27; Num. 18; Deut. 14:22-28; 18. See especially Exod. 23:19 on firstfruits). All of these offerings tied the life of Israel to the stewardship of the land. These offerings to God and care for the poor from the land not only expressed worship to God, but formed the very core of that which kept the Holy Land itself as holy, set apart for God.

- The seventh conception of the land deals with those visions of the prophets in which the land reaches its eschatological fulfillment. These visions are replete with images of the land reaching its ultimate fruition as an idealized expression of God's intention for the land.

In each of these viewpoints, the necessity of stewardship related to the land emerges. The borders of the land call for a stewardship of influence in the midst of the nations. The nature of the land evokes a stewardship of its abundance. The history of the land requires a settlement in the land which fulfills its destiny as the locus of God's mighty acts in history. The promise of the land mandates a response in stewardship that keeps faith with the land thus promised. The conquest of the land requires a stewardship of means to rid the land of that which threatens the purposes of God. The actual living of life in the land, as has been shown, can be addressed principally as a stewardship. Finally, the prophetic vision for the land becomes an *Urzeit-Endzeit* eschatology in which God's promise and human stewardship simultaneously synergize to re-create Eden. Poignant it is that every motif of the land in the Old Testament turns attention back to stewardship.

Fundamental to the idea of Old Testament stewardship is God's outright possession of the land. When prohibiting the sale of the land given to the Hebrews, Yahweh states "the land is mine" (Lev. 25:23). Through invasions the gentile nations have taken over Yahweh's inheritance in the land (Ps. 79:1), the people of Israel defiled the land of God's inheritance (Jer. 2:7), and Yahweh is jealous in God's ownership of the land (Joel 2:18). This emphasis is not merely one of God's real estate interest in the Middle East. As Harper notes:

> The whole relation of the nation and of the individual to the land was raised out of the merely sordid region of material gain into the spiritual and moral region, by the principle that Yahweh their God alone had full proprietary rights over the soil.[7]

From the view of the land as God's possession, typical of the Hebraic inclination for the concrete expression rather than the abstract, there followed an emphasis on all of life as stewardship. That stewardship rooted in the land.

God promised the land to Abraham (Gen. 12:1). When Abraham arrived in the land, God promised that Abraham's posterity would possess that land (Gen. 12:7b). That promise was renewed with Isaac (Gen. 26:3) and Jacob (Gen. 28:13). The land was promised (Deut. 6:3), given (Lev. 20:24), and sworn (Josh. 5:6) to Israel. The realization of that promise in the conquest of the land was likewise the gift and the power of God in the conquest (Josh. 23:3; 2:24).

Essential to an understanding of Old Testament stewardship, however, must be the understanding that God subdivided the ownership of the land to every tribe (Josh. 13-22) and further to every individual man within every tribe (Josh. 24:28). The great idealization of Hebrew history finds expression in the poetic language "And Judah and Israel dwelt safely, each man under his vine and under his fig tree, from Dan as far as Beersheba" (1 Kgs. 4:25). Jer. 12:15 looked beyond the Captivity to the Restoration: "[I will] bring them back, everyone to his heritage, and everyone to his land" (Jer. 12:15). This emphasis has enormous implications for both the Old Testament and contemporary views of stewardship. God not only gives the land to God's people generally, but also portions it out to each head of a family. God did not give the land wholesale to the people. That is, in responsibility to God every individual Hebrew had a portion of God's creation for which to give an accountable stewardship to God. This sense of the individualization of stewardship must underpin all sense of life as a steward of God.

It is also of significance to note the emphasis on other property given to the Hebrew people in addition to the land. Israel received cattle, silver, gold, brass, iron, raiment, vineyards, oliveyards, and fruit trees with the land taken from the Canaanites (Josh. 11:14; 22:8; 24:13). It was said of Hezekiah that "God had given him very much property" (2 Chr. 32:29). Both to royalty and to commoner God had given material wealth other than the land itself.

A complement to the land and other material is the power to get wealth as the gift of God. Moses uses an emphatic expression to underscore Yahweh as the source of the people's ability to get wealth (Deut. 8:17-18). Moses rightly feared that the people would see their conquest of Canaan and the sudden acquisition of wealth by a former slave people as the work of their hands. Further, the *qal* participle in Hebrew indicates that Moses anticipated a continuing divine giving of the power to get wealth, a linear rather than a punctiliar experience. The several Hebrew words for wealth used in the Old Testament indicate that the Hebrews did in fact possess wealth and that this possession was a matter of labor in acquiring the wealth. That is to say that both in an initial way and a continuing way, the power to

generate wealth, value, capital, and equity is a gift from God.
The modern suburbanite considering a stock portfolio, the city
dweller admiring the equity in a condo, or the rancher compla-
cently viewing his land might consider it a mark of achievement. Indeed, it was won by the sweat of his brow. But the very
capacity to achieve wealth has behind it the gift of God.

The promises made to Israel in the Old Testament must not
be exported in a civil religion to the United States, or to any
other nation state. The United States is not the New Israel.
Such distortion belongs to the World Wide Church of God in
the British Israelism of Herbert W. and Garner Ted Armstrong.
Then in what way does the stewardship of the land relate to
where contemporary Christians are physically located?
Christian stewards must translate the stewardship of Old
Testament Israel into terms of life today in the concreteness of
our own lives. While acknowledging that we do not live in the
promised land, we nevertheless live out our stewardship in a
place of which we are the stewards under God. Our borders are
a place of influence, abundance, history, and promise. We have
a stewardship to conquer that which dehumanizes life and renders it unsacred. We must live in our place and time with ecological responsibility that does not exploit and with stewardship
of the resources of the land for the work of God's Kingdom.
And we must keep the bright vision of a land that keeps faith
with God's promise for tomorrow. If we do not understand it in
terms of a civil religion, there is nothing wrong and much right
with the stirring words of "America"; the biblical promise
echoes in the hope:

> Thine alabaster cities gleam
> Undimmed by human tears.

The cynic will quickly respond that our rust-belt cities are anything but alabaster and that human tears flow in the streets of drug-infested ghettoes. Christians must live with that same stewardship of promise that holds possible the transformation of society under the lordship of Christ. That is the modern equivalent of Israel's stewardship of the promise.

Worship as a Means of Stewardship

Hebrew worship centered first in the Tabernacle and then in the Temple. The covenant called for a certain people, place, offering, and time of worship. In the patriarchal times the patriarchs themselves acted in priestly ways. The formal priesthood as an ordained institution began with the consecration of Levi and his sons. The priests had the primary stewardship for the religious life of Israel, its traditions and rituals. That life centered around the place of the Tabernacle and then the Temple. In a very real sense the priests led all Israel in a stewardship of that place. The tragic civil war resulted in a divided kingdom centered in part around a division of the places of worship between Jerusalem and the shrine in the North.

At the center of worship rested the sacrificial system of Israel. Leviticus takes great pains to describe that sacrificial system, listing the names, purposes, types, and portions of the sacrifice given to God, priests, and worshiper. Yet nowhere do the Old Testament writers present a precise theology of sacrifice. Why then did the sacrificial system become the centerpiece of Old Testament life? First, the sacrifices were a gift to Yahweh. That a person would appear in God's presence with empty hands, without a gift, was utterly foreign to the Hebrew. One can safely say that in the center of the Old Testament view of sacrifice the aspect of gift predominated. The modern practice of appearing at church and never giving to the offering would have surprised the ancient Hebrew as much as a Martian landing in the Tabernacle. There was no such thing as appearing before the Lord with empty hands.

The prevailing idea of sacrifice in the Old Testament appears to have been that of a gift to God.[8] Even the sacrifice of Cain and Abel was called in Hebrew a "present." That sacrifice involved the willing giving of a gift to God rests at the foundation of Old Testament stewardship.

Yet at the same time the gifts were no mere mechanical offering to placate a remote deity. The Old Testament makes it clear that the gifts were intended as a means for communion with Yahweh. When the Hebrew worshiper selected the best animal from his flock, laboriously carried the animal to the altar, and heaved it up as an act of physical surrender to Yahweh, the entire process involved a new depth of communion with God. It was no mere *ex opere operata* view of sacrifice. As the scented smoke of a sacrifice wafted its way to heaven, it carried with it a new communion with Yahweh.

At the heart of the sacrificial system was an intent to atone for sin. The burnt offering, sin offering, and trespass offering were intended to atone for the sins of the worshiper. Although no definite provision was made for "sins of the high hand," i.e., deliberate sins, nevertheless, provision was made for sins unknowingly committed. Yet at the heart of each purpose in the offering rested the stewardship of the people. The offering as gift to Yahweh represented the people's sense of trusteeship pure and simple. The offering as a means to communion demonstrated that stewardship itself was an occasion if not a bridge for communion with God. To commune with the God who gave so much, the worshiper met that God in a communion of giving which reflected the giving of God. Even in the atonement for sin, an act of God's pure grace, the atonement took place in the midst of an offering for sin reflective of the stewardship of the offerer.

A more detailed description of the sacrificial system demonstrates the relationship between the sacrificial system and stewardship principles that abide. A review of the offerings and their purposes repays theological reflection:

The Burnt Offering (Heb. *'olāh* Lev. 1:1-17; 6:8-13). In this oblation, the entire animal was burned on the altar as a "pleasing odor to Yahweh." This sacrifice was voluntary in nature, at the discretion of the worshiper. The purpose was a propitiation for sin (Lev. 1:4) and an act of total dedication to Yahweh, even as the sacrifice was wholly consumed on the altar. The offering was to be given in proportion to one's wealth: bull, sheep, goat, turtledove, or pigeon. The consumption of this offering in the conflagration of the altar fire symbolized a completeness of devotion to God. There is not a specific time at which the offering is to be given by an individual. It was part of all major corporate worship activities and was offered twice daily on behalf of the nation as a whole. It was doubled on the Sabbath.

Timeless principles of stewardship inhere in this prototype of giving. At its best, our giving to God is a voluntary act. Coerced giving, whether by a state church or through spiritual manipulation, does not reflect the standard of biblical stewardship. When the Israelite brought the burnt offering, it came from an inward compulsion, not an outward coercion. The consumption of the gift in its entirety on the altar represents that attitude which gives and backs away from the gift, leaving it all in the hands of God. There is a way of giving which seeks to hold on to the gift even in the giving, to control or to dominate the use of the gift itself. In the fire of the altar, the gift belongs to God alone. At the same time, such stewardship represents the total gift of the worshiper to God. There was no mechanical separation between the giver and the gift, as if the giver had taken care of a religious obligation and might go to live as he pleased. No, in the burnt offering the giver symbolized the giving of self to God. The best giving is always that giving in which the gift represents the giving of the worshiper to God, not just the gift.

The Grain Offering (Heb. *minḥāh* Lev. 2:1-16; 6:14-18; 7:12-13). This offering of flour, oil, spice, or grain and spice—sometimes cooked into cakes—was offered with the burnt offering. A portion was burned on the altar but the remainder was eaten by the priests in the court of the Tabernacle. This voluntary offering demonstrated reverence and thanksgiving toward God. It demonstrated the principle that gifts to God can come from more than one source. Not only the living animals were brought to the altar, but also the grain cultivated in the field. The worshiper can approach God with anything that represents value as an expression of the investment in life. Not only the shepherd with his staff but the farmer with his scythe can bring to God the work of his hands.

Further, this offering demonstrates the stewardship of support for the ministry as an institution. From time immemorial, God has elected that certain believers be set aside for ministry in God's institutions. They are not better than other believers, but they are different in that they devote all of life as a professional vocation to the service of God's institutions. It is right that they be supported by the gifts of those to whom they minister. This principle roots in the deepest strata of biblical revelation. When this privilege is abused, as it was in the medieval benefices and sinecures, it does not reflect proper use of stewardship. When this support is received appropriately and used wisely and prudently by the ministers thus supported, it frees the ministry to be the servant of God's people. As one hardworking southern preacher who loved his flock sacrificially related, "I serve elderly ladies whose hands bleed on the white bowls of cotton they pick in order to tithe to our church; I can do no less than be the most faithful to them."

The Peace Offering (Heb. *zebaḥ šelem* Lev. 3:1-17; 7:11-21, 28-34). According to the worshiper's means, this was a bull or cow, a sheep, or a goat. This was the most common of the offerings. It was an expression of thanksgiving to God for divine intervention or deliverance; or a votive offering after a vow had been kept. The blood, fat, and internal organs representing life were burned on the altar for Yahweh. The remainder of the animal was eaten by the worshipers in the court of the Tabernacle. This implied that they were guests at Yahweh's table, or God was a guest at theirs.

There were three classes of peace offerings:

- The first class was the thank offering, which was to express a certain devotion of mind, and had the significance primarily of a gift or present to God. Whenever one had received an answer to prayer, he was not to appear before God empty-handed.
- The second class of peace offering was the vow offering. This was an offering given after the reception of some benefit sought from God.
- The third class, the freewill offering, was nothing but a self-determined act of desire to give to God for no other reason than the thankful sense of the worshiper.

In the peace offering, we see a beautiful illustration of stewardship principles. Our gifts to God can be motivated out of God's goodness in our lives. How many times God has intervened in life, emergency, illness, and stress to carry believers through. Stewardship in the wake of such events is an appropriate expression to God of gratitude for divine intervention. Such giving should be a spontaneous, natural outflow of a worshiper's heart. It is unnatural, perverse, and subhuman not to feel such an impulse in the face of God's mighty acts for an individual. Here rests also the biblical roots for the joyful celebrative aspect of giving to God. When the Hebrew families gathered to share the meal of the peace offering in the presence of God and one another, it was an occasion of joy. It was a solemn and joyful occasion in which worship blended into communion with one another as well as communion with God.

The Sin Offering (Heb. *ḥaṭā't* Leviticus 4). This offering made right the relationship of the offerer with God. It could have been a young bullock, male goat, female goat, female lamb, two doves, or one-tenth ephah of flour. This offering still had the quality of a stewardship gift:

> If the bearing of punishment by the victim were the leading idea, then in no case, not even in a case of poverty, would a vegetable offering be allowable. That this is possible proves that the essence of the act is not the death penalty, but the gift.[9]

The Trespass Offering (Heb. *'āšām*, Lev. 5:14-16). This concerns an individual who had committed a trespass against a neighbor or in the things concerning Yahweh. The guilty party would bring a ram and make restitution to the party wronged.

In summary, the Old Testament presents sacrifice as a form of stewardship on the part of God's people. Prior to Moses, the offerings were simple and few. Cain, Abel, Noah, Abraham,

Isaac, Jacob, and others sought to be at harmony with God through the giving of sacrifices. Through Moses, Yahweh gave to the Hebrews an elaborate sacrificial system which required considerable use of property. At times, such as the dedication of Solomon's Temple, sacrifices were abundantly given (1 Kgs. 8:62-63). After Hezekiah's cleansing of the Temple, the feast of Passover was extended to twice its usual length with abundant offerings (2 Chronicles 30). At the dedication of the second Temple, offerings were abundant (Ezra 6:16-17).

VARIOUS OTHER OLD TESTAMENT OFFERINGS

Other aspects of stewardship through offering characterize the Old Testament patterns of giving. Taken together, these demonstrate the rich texture of stewardship in the Old Testament as it touched every area of life.

The Offering of the Firstborn. Num. 3:13 states " ... because all the firstborn are Mine. On the day that I struck all the first-born in the land of Egypt, I sanctified to Myself all the firstborn in Israel, both man and beast. They shall be Mine: I am the Lord." In reaction to the divine command to Moses, Israel was to set aside all firstborn (Exod. 13:2; 13:13; Deut. 15:19). Of course, Israel did not practice the actual sacrifice of firstborn human males. They were redeemed at five shekels each. This practice of giving the firstborn recognized that life itself is the gift of God. It further underscored the stewardship involved in receiving and giving back to God the gift of life. It reached its highest expression in the sacrifice of the "only begotten" Son of God on the Cross (John 3:16). As Oesterley observed, "Other purposes were undoubtedly included in the sacrifice of the first-born of the flocks and herds...but they were, in the first instance, gifts to the deity."[10] In a larger sense, the offering of the firstborn recognized that all of life's significant passages represented occasions in which gifts should be given to God.

The Offering of Firstfruits. To the Hebrew, the appearance of the firstfruits evidenced the direct intervention of God (Deut. 26:10). In a land where everything depended upon the early and latter rains, the Hebrew farmer looked to the heavens above for the rain that brought life or the absence of which threatened life. In such an agrarian culture, the appearance of the firstfruits marked an event awaited by the entire community. Because of this, the firstfruits were considered to be holy (Lev. 23:20; Ezek. 48:14). The farmer was to bring the firstfruits from all the increase of his field (Prov. 3:9; 2 Chr. 31:5). This involved grain, new wine, and oil (Num. 18:12). Sometimes this involved honey (2 Chr. 31:5) and dough or coarse meal (Num. 15:17-21). In the same context the first fleece of the sheep was also offered to God (Deut. 18:4).

The practice of giving the first and the best to God functioned as a cornerstone of Hebrew giving. As an abiding principle it calls for a stewardship that does not give God life's leftovers but rather the first and the best of one's efforts. Today the principle expresses itself in giving to God from that which comes at the beginning of an endeavor, out of the first profits from an endeavor rather than only the last. In a professional or business world where "net profit" or the "bottom line" might be manipulated in many ways, it would be possible at the end of any process to find nothing left to give God. The practice of firstfruit giving remembers God from the first.

The Fruit of the Fourth Year. When the Hebrews came into the promised land, they were to plant it with various fruit trees.

For three years these trees were to be treated as "uncircumcised," that is, they were not to be eaten (Lev. 19:23). On the fourth year the fruit was to be offered to God as a symbol of God's fructifying powers. Only in the fifth year were the people to eat of the fruit: "And in the fifth year you may eat its fruit, that it may yield to you its increase: I am the Lord your God" (Lev. 19:25). As an abiding principle, this recognized the developmental and maturing nature of God's blessings in life. So much that comes to believers requires the process of God's blessing year after year. In the offering of the fourth year's fruit to the Lord, the worshiper demonstrated a trust in God's ongoing provision and acknowledged that trust in a giving to God. In an age where fruit could sometimes be a relative rarity, it was an act of trust to consecrate the fruit to God for an entire year.

The Drink Offering. With the burnt offering, a libation or liquid offering of wine was offered, varying with the quality of the burnt offering, a diminishing amount being given with a bull, a ram, or a lamb (Num. 28:14). The fruit of the vine bore a special relationship to Israel, the grape cluster itself a symbol in both ancient and modern Israel. The vine in a sense represented the blessings of God on Israel. The aggregate life of the people was offered back to God in the libation offering poured out on the burnt offering. It was an offering above and beyond the animal offering, a final and crowning act in which the very vitality represented by the vine complemented the animal sacrifice. It was, in this sense, a luxuriant offering of life itself back to God.

The Wood Offering. This offering was not mentioned until the time of Nehemiah (10:34). The enormous offerings given at the Temple required a proportionately large amount of wood to consume the sacrifices. The giving of this wood would represent a real sacrifice in a land often denuded of wood by invaders and hardly larger than the state of Vermont. The giving of wood indicates a willingness on the part of the worshiper to enable the entire system of sacrificial offering.

The Spoils of War Offering. Abraham gave to the priest Melchizedek a tithe of the spoil taken in the war against the kings (Gen. 14:20). In the conquest of Jericho, the precious metals of the conquered city were given to the treasury of Yahweh (Josh. 6:24). In the confrontation with Sennacherib, booty was brought to Jerusalem for the purposes of Yahweh (2 Chr. 32:23). This reflects the necessity to remember the role of God in the victories of life, the conquests that evidence the power of God in the battle.

STEWARDSHIP FOR THE CONSTRUCTION OF TABERNACLE AND TEMPLE

Another major category of Old Testament giving was that centered in the construction of the Tabernacle and the Temple, as well as the refurbishing of the Temple after it had fallen into disrepair or disuse.

Sacrificial Stewardship for Building the Tabernacle

The first occasion of sacrificial giving for the construction of God's house was the construction of the Tabernacle. Above all, this giving was an act of worship to Yahweh. The offering was for Yahweh (Exod. 25:2), unto Yahweh (Exod. 35:5, 22, 29), and Yahweh's offering (Exod. 35:21, 24). Grounded in this passage is the essence of giving as an act of worship to God. There is no primary emphasis on the erection of an edifice. Although that was the occasion of this giving, central throughout is the emphasis on giving as an act of worship to God.

An unmistakable mark of this giving was a "willing heart" (Exod. 35:5). Those who gave were everyone "whose heart was stirred, and everyone whose spirit was willing" (Exod. 35:21). Giving for special construction did not begin with a coercive appeal. God wanted the people to give only what God always wants them to give, that which their hearts moved them to give. In that regard giving was not an outward compulsion but an inward propulsion from a willing heart. Just as the sunlight naturally melts ice, causes a flower to open its petals, and awakens a slumbering baby, the goodness of God creates a willing heart. The people gave with an abundance that created an unusual necessity. Moses had to restrain the people from giving more (Exod. 36:2-7).

It is not often in the history of God's people that the minister must say, "Stop the offering!" There was more than enough given to meet the need for the construction of God's house. A wide variety of gifts comprised this offering. Personal items of great value were given, including bracelets, earrings, rings, tablets, and jewels (Exod. 35:22), blue, purple, scarlet cloths, fine linen, goat's hair, ram skins, badger skins, silver, brass, shittimwood, spun cloth, onyx, spice, oil, and other valuable commodities (Exod. 35:22-29). Some of these gifts represent what only the poorest could find, the hair of a goat. Yet also represented were the offerings that could be brought by the most affluent. It was a comprehensive offering by the people of God in every life situation.

At the conclusion of this process, God validated the gifts of the people with a theophany: "Then the cloud covered the tabernacle of meeting, and the glory of the Lord filled the tabernacle" (Exod. 40:34). The outcome of the people's stewardship was the visible presence of God with the people at the tent of meeting. Here was the presence of God in the midst of a willing, sacrificial, inclusive act of stewardship on the part of God's people. The abiding principle indicates the pleasure God takes when the people so give in the times of special need for God's work and house.

Sacrificial Stewardship for Building the Temple

The next auspicious, unusual offering for constructing the house of God came with the construction of the Temple. David led the way by committing vast personal resources to the construction. He gave gold, silver, brass, iron, wood, onyx, precious stones, and marble (1 Chr. 29:2-5). Following the example of David, other leaders of the nation at several ranks (fathers, princes, captains, and rulers) also gave sacrificial gifts for the construction (1 Chr. 29:6). In a magnificent prayer of praise David hallowed God for God's greatness. He acknowledged that the source of both wealth and strength is God (1 Chr. 29:12). Then David made one of the single most instructive confessions concerning stewardship in the Old Testament:

> But who am I, and who are my people, that we should be able to offer so willingly as this? For all things come from You. And of Your own we have given You… O Lord our God, all this abundance that we have prepared to build You a house for Your holy name is from Your hand, and is all Your own (1 Chr. 29:14, 16).

In this confession, David moved beyond any sense of obligation in stewardship to a confession of amazement that God would condescend to allow the people to give back to God that which was already God's anyway. It is an absolute acknowledgment of God's ownership of all things and human dependence upon God even in the act of giving. Few verses better state the highest realm of stewardship theology in the Old Testament. Emphasis rests repeatedly on the willingness with which the people gave and the great joy that flooded the congregation. Absent is any indication of the coercive or onerous. Present is a moving scene of national corporate worship on this occasion. Once again, the glory of Yahweh filled the building (2 Chr. 7:1-3) at the time of dedication.

Giving for the Repair of the Temple under Jehoash and Josiah

On two occasions, the Temple of Solomon was repaired. The first of these occurred under Jehoash (2 Kgs. 12:4-15; 2 Chr. 24:4-14). Money for this repair came from three sources:
- there was a tax of a half-shekel mentioned by Moses in the building of the Tabernacle;
- money was collected in the payment of vows;
- there was a freewill offering.

The king commanded that the priest Jehoida make a chest and place it in the Temple. The priests placed the money into the chest and the program of giving was successful for the repair of the Temple. The repair of the Temple under Josiah is not given so elaborate a treatment, but the scheme of stewardship must have been similar (2 Kgs. 22:3-7).

Giving for the Rebuilding of the Temple in the Days of Ezra

The peculiar aspect of this stewardship was the "stirring" of the heart of Cyrus, the Persian king, to lead in rebuilding the Temple of the Jews (Ezra 1:1-4). Precious metals, goods, and beasts were to be given to the Jews to assist them in their return journey. Beyond this, a freewill offering was to be given for building God's house. This command was targeted at non-Israelites. Darius expanded this decree (Ezra 6:3-12) and Artaxerxes likewise participated (Ezra 7:20-22). It is likely that these efforts also included the Jews who remained in the Captivity.

This experience has several implications for the development of a universal concept of stewardship. God can call upon the resources of those who are not even God's own people. The wealth of the nations belongs to God, who is able to stir them to use that wealth for divine purposes. This can further be seen in the experience of Nehemiah, to whom Artaxerxes gave letters of credit for the rebuilding of the walls of Jerusalem (Neh. 2:7-8). When the necessity presents itself, God can move the hearts of pure pagans for the support of God's work. This implies a universal opportunity for stewardship and further suggests that when God's people are unable or unwilling to support God's work on the Earth, God can find other channels to do so.

STEWARDSHIP AS CHARITABLE GIVING IN THE OLD TESTAMENT

By the nature of the covenant community, Old Testament giving embraced the needy and the less fortunate. The objects of Hebrew charity included the poor, the sojourners, the fatherless or orphans, the widows, and the Levites. During the first six years of the sabbatical cycle, several provisions were made for the needy. The corners of the fields were not to be reaped but rather left for the poor (Lev. 19:9-10; 23:22). The same was true of the gleanings from the fields (Lev. 19:9-10; 23:22; Deut. 24:19). The vineyards were not to be gleaned, and fallen fruit from the vineyards was to be left on the ground for the poor (Lev. 19:10). The olive groves were not to be thrashed a second time so that some of the fruit would be left for the poor. In the feasts of Weeks and

Booths, the poor were to share in the freewill offerings of the more affluent (Deut. 16:10, 11, 14). In the sabbatical year, debts were to be forgiven and slaves released. The released slave was to be provided with resources to begin life (Deut. 15:1-4, 12-14). Likewise, in the sabbatical year, volunteer crops from the fallow land, vineyard, and olive groves were to be left for the poor (Exod. 23:10-11).

PRINCIPLES FROM OLD TESTAMENT STEWARDSHIP

Obviously, for this comprehensive study, those timeless principles which transcend the local circumstances of Old Testament stewardship must be identified. To move from the time and place specific to the timeless and universal generalization is the essential hermeneutic move in the interpretation of Old Testament stewardship teaching. Several aspects of Old Testament giving lend themselves to such generalization and transcend the immediate to become part of the ultimate in stewardship.

Stewardship is an Act of Worship. Stewardship grows out of an encounter with God. From the earliest gifts of Cain and Abel, the act of stewardship originates in an encounter with God. Noah encountered the power of God in an awesome salvation of his family from the flood. His response was to build an altar and give to God (Gen. 8:20). Abraham's experience of God's call, leadership, rebuke, and providence moved him throughout his life to respond with altar and sacrifice. Jacob encountered God in his famous Jabok experience of angels ascending and descending. Out of this encounter with God, Jacob made his vow to tithe (Gen. 28:20-22).

51

The Hebrews who gave to Yahweh in the wake of the Exodus had seen the mighty acts of God in the ten plagues, the parting of the Red Sea, the inundation of the Egyptian army, and God's miraculous provision of food and water. As God reminded them, "You have seen what I did to the Egyptians, and how I bore you on eagles' wings and brought you to Myself" (Exod. 19:4). It was particularly out of the experience of God's mighty acts that the Hebrews responded with giving.

In the latter part of the Old Testament the renewal of giving grew out of a renewed encounter with God. The resumption of tithing at the time of Hezekiah's revival grew out of a renewed experience with God (2 Chr. 31:12). The resumption of tithing under Nehemiah reflected the providence of God in the return of the people from the Captivity and the rebuilding of Jerusalem (Neh. 13:10-13). In a negative way, Malachi connects the absence of the tithe to a withered and atrophied relationship with God, which resulted in God's curse on the people (Mal. 3:8).

In the five instances of giving for the construction or reconstruction of places of worship, the entire ambiance of the occasion speaks of a renewed encounter with God and a desire to worship God in a sacrificial provision for the house of God. As in all instances of Old Testament stewardship, giving grows out of and in turn leads to a renewed relationship with God.

Stewardship is a Spirit of Willingness. A key concept of Old Testament stewardship is the theme of freewill offerings. The Hebrew radical thus translated suggests "to impel or to incite." Thirteen times this expression is used in the *hithpael* to express showing oneself to be willing. This quality of freewill offering described not only the regular giving but also the extraordinary giving of the Hebrew people. In the giving for the construction of the Tabernacle and Temple, it is especially underscored that the people gave only as the Lord moved their hearts to give. The irony of contradicting freewill offerings belonged to the scathing rebuke of Amos, who ridiculed those who proclaimed the legal necessity of freewill offerings, thus setting up a contradiction in terms. To order someone to do what they must do voluntarily for the act to have meaning is absurd (Amos 4:5).

Stewardship Expresses Itself in the Spirit of Sacrifice. From the example of Abraham's willingness to sacrifice Isaac, that which was dearest to him, the underlying motif of much Old Testament giving was that of sacrifice. Central to giving was the emphasis on self-denial, that which cost the giver from the substance of life. For the average Hebrew peasant farmer to take one-tenth of his substance, not to mention the best of the flock, and render this to God involved a radical commitment to sacrifice. The essence of this sacrificial concept is expressed in David's refusal to receive Ornan's threshing floor as a gift which would have provided a free place for worship. David's refusal to offer to God that which had come at no cost to him demonstrates the necessity of the sacrificial spirit in giving to God (1 Chr. 21:24). To give in such a way that one's lifestyle is changed characterizes Old Testament giving.

Stewardship Relates to an Individual's Ability to Give. Recognized throughout the Old Testament is the varying ability of people to give. In the standard sacrificial offerings, animals of diminishing value were permitted based on the individual's ability to give. On the special occasions of stewardship, there was also a marked emphasis on the ability of the giver. However, that providence of God had enriched an individual was reflected in the quality of and expense of the offering to be brought. No one was expected to give beyond reasonable ability. Therefore, the poorer gift of the needy person was as acceptable to God as the more elaborate gift of the affluent person.

Stewardship Relates to Spiritual Health and Personal Relationships. In the first recorded act of giving, Abel gave acceptably because of his faith in God. In some way the gift of Cain lacked that quality (Gen. 4:1-8; Heb. 11:4). When Saul failed to obey God in the matter of the Amalekites, his disobedience affected the acceptance of his offering (1 Sam. 15:22). Faith which issues in obedience conditions stewardship. In his great penitential psalm, David correlated acceptable sacrifice with a spirit of humility before God (Ps. 51:17-19). In a famous statement, Hosea connected a right motive with giving which is acceptable to God: "For I desire mercy, and not sacrifice, and the knowledge of God more than burnt offerings" (Hos. 6:6). Amos particularly emphasized the necessity for right relationship with other men in giving of gifts to God. As he speaks for Yahweh, Amos complains, "I hate, I despise your feast days, and I do not savor your sacred assemblies" (Amos 5:21). This is in the context of injustices done to the poor among the Israelites.

Stewardship Takes Place in a Context of Rejoicing. The element of joy so permeates the giving of the Old Testament that it can be considered a principle of such giving. In those offerings where the people were to eat before Yahweh at the place of worship, there was an injunction to rejoice (Deut. 12:5-7, 17-18; 14:26; 16:11, 13-14; cf. Lev. 23:40). When David had gathered the materials for the Temple there was an outpouring of joy (1 Chr. 29:9, 17). In the offering of the chest of Jehoash both the priests and the people rejoiced (2 Chr. 24:9-10). Under Ezra the rebuilding of the Temple was observed with joy (Ezra 6:16-17). After Nehemiah had finished the rebuilding of the wall, there was a time of sacrifice accompanied by great joy (Neh. 12:43). It is clear that on regular occasions of giving as well as those extraordinary times of stewardship the people responded with a sense of spontaneous joy.

STEWARDSHIP OF THE MISSION

In the largest sense, Israel had the stewardship of God's mission to all humanity. The tension between universalism and particularism in the Old Testament rests beyond the scope of this book. Yet a brief discussion of the mission for which Israel was to be God's steward in the Earth is appropriate. In the call of Abraham is the hint of that worldwide mission: "In you all the families of the Earth shall be blessed" (Gen. 12:3). The Hebrew might actually express that all the families of the Earth will bless themselves because of what God is doing in the call of Abraham. In one way or the other this is repeated in Gen. 18:18, 22:18, 26:4, and 28:14. It was recognized that in the covenant made with Abraham, God was acting in such a way as to bless all humanity. The development of this throughout the Old Testament was as certain as it was slow in its full and profound revelation.

In the great prayer which Solomon prayed at the dedication of the Temple, there was a recognition that part of the Temple's purpose was "that all peoples of the earth may know Your name, and fear You, as do Your people Israel, and that they may know that this temple which I have built is called by Your name" (I Kgs. 8:43). Isa. 56:6-7 envisions a day when the gentile world will be drawn to Jerusalem and the Temple. This resulted in Jesus' quotation from the same passage: "My house shall be called a house of prayer for all nations" (Mark 11:17; cf. Matt. 21:13; Luke 19:46). In the words of H. H. Rowley:

In all these passages we find the thought of Jerusalem as the great religious centre of the world. It is not alone believed that the nations will come to share Israel's faith and worship Israel's God, but Israel herself shall be in the centre of the picture, and the Temple shall be looked to by all men as the religious headquarters of the world.[11]

As this stewardship of God's missionary intention enlarges, Isaiah echoes the intent that Israel's election includes her mandate to call all the world to Yahweh:

I, the Lord, have called you in righteousness, and will hold your hand; I will keep you and give you as a covenant to the people, as a light to the Gentiles, to open blind eyes, to bring out prisoner from the prison, those who sit in darkness for the prison house. I am the Lord, that is My name; And My glory I will not give to another, Nor My praise to carved images (Isa. 42:6-8).

Here Israel has an active mission to reach out to the benighted and spiritually imprisoned gentile world to guide them to the truth of God. This emphasis reached its peak in the so-called servant songs of Isaiah, an exegesis of which is beyond the scope of this book. Suffice it to say that Israel did have the stewardship of a missionary message to the world. That emerges in the late Old Testament books of Ruth and Jonah. The universalism of God's purposes sweeps up the Moabitess Ruth into the purposes of God so that she becomes an ancestor of both David and the Messiah. Jonah goes to preach a message of repentance to the hated city of Nineveh, a reluctant evangelist in a remarkable revival of a pagan city. That Israel had a mission to the world rings clear in the latter stages of the Old Testament. Yet they failed to be stewards of that message. During the intertestamental period a narrowness, exclusivism, and isolation cut them off from that mission. Finally, that mission was taken up by one born from among the Jews, the Lord Jesus Christ, born Son of the Jewess Mary and of the Holy Spirit—a Jewish Savior for the entire world.

Chapter Three

———◦◦◦———

The Tithe in the Old Testament

T he extent and the influence of the tithe in the Old Testament calls for a separate treatment. S. R. Driver has stated that there is not enough information at our disposal to write a history of the Hebrew tithe.[1] There is, however, sufficient information to gather an assessment of tithing. Before treating the biblical materials, it is significant to contrast and compare material from the ancient world as it relates to the proportion given to the gods as a matter of common practice.

TITHING IN THE ANCIENT WORLD

Lansdell investigated in the greatest historical detail the practice of ancient Egyptians, Semites, Greeks, and Romans with regard to tithing.[2] Nearly a century later, no one has gone beyond the research of this monumental work in gathering primary resources. It was clear from an inscription at Lycopolis dating circa 2500 BC that the inhabitants of the Nile Valley dedicated the firstfruits of the harvest to the deity.[3] Maspero indicates that some Egyptians practiced the giving of a tenth of the spoil after a military victory.[4] Under the Ptolemies it appears that the "god's" portion was one-sixth, paid to the nearest temple of a god from lands, orchards, and vineyards.[5] The Tel-el-Amarna cuneiform tablets confirm that a tenth part of a person's increase was sometimes given to the gods of Babylon. Sayce, Professor of Assyriology at Oxford, considered the "tithe" a Babylonian institution, paid to the temples from the produce of the land.[6]

The tithe was paid by all classes and mostly paid in corn. Further, Cyrus and Cambyses considered it necessary to pay a tithe to the gods of the kingdoms they had conquered.[7] The Persians offered a tenth of the spoil taken after any campaign to their deities. The Phoenicians founded Carthage and sent a tithe of all increases back to Tyre.[8] Among ancient Arabians, there was a law that required them to give a tithe of incense to the god Sabis. Baal worship also required the donation of certain tithes.[9] The ancient Ethiopians were said by Pliny to give as much as one-third of their cinnamon to the sun god. Thus, throughout the ancient Near East, the practice of the tithe characterized much if not all of religious giving. Among the Greeks, soldiers serving under Agamemnon were said to have consecrated a tenth of the goods taken from the Mycenaens.[10] Clement of Alexandria, as an aside, indicates that at Delphi there were pillars on which worshipers would hang up their tithes. Pisistratus replied to Solon that certain princes had taken a tithe for the gods and profaned it by their own personal use, a strong testimony to the sacred quality of the tenth in ancient Greece.[11] Among the Spartans Agesilaus, king of Sparta, as well as generals Pausanius and Agesilaus, gave tithes after battle. Cimon of Athens dedicated a tenth of the spoils of battle to "god" after defeating the Persians. Herodotus mentioned numerous examples of tithing by people under the hegemony of the Hellenic empire.[12] Xenophon in Anabasis recalls that retreating Greeks gave a tenth of the money they got from the sale of captives to Apollo and Diana. Xenophon built a temple to Diana on the road from Lacedaemon to Olympia to which annually a tenth from the surrounding land was to be given. The temple was endowed with tithes for the support of the priests and the repair of the temple.[13] Later, Demosthenes wrote of the sacrilege in some cities where the tenth belonging to the gods was not paid.[14] The testimony of Hellenic Greece indicates that payment of tithes was normal and not extraordinary.

In the earliest legendary history of Rome, rulers tithed.[15] The reverence given to tithes by both Greeks and Romans was indicated in an account given by both Livy and Plutarch. After the conquest of Veii by Camillus (395 BC), the Augurs reported that the deities were offended because a tithe had not been given. Money from the Roman treasury was given to rectify this oversight by sending the money to Delphi to be offered to Apollo. The delegation carrying the offering was intercepted by pirates. When the pirates learned of the sacred character of the mission, they entertained the tithe carriers and sent them with protection on their way.[16] This anecdote reveals the universal reverence in which the tithe was held in the ancient world. That a similar portion was given by the Gauls, Britons, and German Saxons was recorded by Julius Caesar and others.[17] A survey of the ancient world surrounding the biblical peoples indicated a pervasive sense of giving a tenth to the gods. This existed over such an extensive area of geography and a similar extensive period of time that it rests beyond serious question that giving a tenth or more of life's increase was almost universally a practice of ancient peoples. In that regard, the biblical peoples belonged not to the exception but to the rule among ancient peoples at the point of tithing.

TITHING AMONG THE PATRIARCHS

Abraham and Jacob are the first two biblical characters explicitly named as giving a tithe. The instances that led to these proto-tithing episodes are instructive. In some ways, Genesis 14 is the strangest chapter in the cycle of narratives concerning Abraham. He is introduced in verse 13 as "Abraham the Hebrew" as if he were for some reason being introduced for the first time. Abraham was drawn into an ancient territorial skirmish among chieftains in the Palestinian area. Four kings of the East marched westward to confront five petty rulers whose fiefdoms were south of the Dead Sea. After defeating the five chieftains, the four from the East captured Lot, Abraham's nephew. With 318 men, Abraham chased them and defeated them in the area of Damascus. Abraham was met on the return by the King of Sodom and the Priest-King Melchizedek. This mysterious priest from the area around Jerusalem met Abraham with bread and wine to refresh him on the long trek home. He blessed Abraham for his unselfish act in rescuing his nephew. With no elaborate introduction—indeed as almost an incidental statement—Genesis records "he gave him a tithe of all" (Gen. 14:20). There was no objection from any of Abraham's fellow soldiers in the battle. Why would Abraham have rendered this portion with so little fanfare or note? Professor Sayce indicates:

> This offering of tithes was no new thing. In his Babylonian home, Abraham must have been familiar with the practice. The cuneiform inscriptions of Babylonia contain frequent references

to it. It went back to the pre-Semitic age of Chaldea, and the great temples of Babylonia were largely supported by the *esra*, or tithe, which was levied upon prince and peasant alike. That the god should receive a tenth of the good things, which it was believed he had bestowed upon mankind, was not considered to be asking too much. There are many tablets in the British Museum which are receipts for the payment of the tithe to the great temple of the sun god at Sippara, in the time of Nebuchadnezzar and his successors.[18]

It is of note that Abraham was willing to surrender to other humans whatever interest they had in the nine-tenths that were not to be given to God, but he clearly indicated that he was not in a position to dispose to humans that which was to be given to God. In all likelihood this was not an exceptional act on Abraham's part. He lived within a day of Melchizedek's location at Salem (Jerusalem) and one could only suppose that it was the habit of Abraham to give tithes as did his Mesopotamian ancestors. Tithing on the part of Abraham brings overwhelming weight to the ongoing practice of giving the tenth. Abraham is the first person whose faith is specifically mentioned in the Bible. He is the great exemplar and prototype of all those who live and walk by faith. It goes without saying that the three great monotheistic religions all look back to Abraham: Judaism, Christianity, and Islam. His life and acts have been considered the foundation of the life of faith by generations of believers. The practice of tithing by the patriarch lifts it out of the realm of "legalistic" discussion. By all means it removes it from a discussion of the applicability of the Mosaic Law for Christians. Before Moses, Exodus, or the later codification of the Jewish law, the great Nestor of the biblical faith gave tithes as naturally as he breathed. The very incidental way in which his practice was introduced demonstrates the expected, common, and natural expectation that a person of faith was to tithe. Against the backdrop of tithing in the ancient pagan world, it would have been a travesty for Abraham to have done less.

Jacob, the grandson of Abraham, reveals the second explicit mention of tithing in the Old Testament. It can be inferred that his father, Isaac, also practiced giving the tithe. At any rate, Abraham lived until the boyhood of Jacob. If for some unknown reason Isaac omitted to tithe, Jacob would have heard from the venerable patriarch the story of Abraham's own tithing experience. In all likelihood, the practice of the tithe had carried through the generations of the family. Faced with the rage of Esau, Jacob fled the family home and headed to Haran. On the first night of the journey he stopped at the ancient site of Luz and slept under the star-studded firmament. Alone, haunted by the past, isolated in the present, and fearful of the future, he fell into a troubled sleep with his head resting on a stone. How different from the sumptuous tented city of his patriarch father and grandfather with 318 servants to meet every need. In the depth of sleep he dreamed of his famous ladder with God at the top and angelic messengers ascending and descending. God renewed the covenant with Abraham making it personal to Jacob. The very land which Jacob was fleeing would be given to him according to the covenant. His descendants would cover the points of the compass and all humanity would be blessed through them (Gen. 28:10-15).

Jacob awoke to acknowledge the presence of God and expressed reverential awe at the theophany he had witnessed. A place of common life had suddenly turned into a gate of heaven. His response to the revelation was fourfold. He erected an altar from his stone pillow. He offered oil on the altar as an act of worship. He renamed Bethel, the house of God. After the encounter with God and the worship related to it, he made a vow to tithe. Some have impeached his vow as a cheap bargaining with God. In the context of the revelation and with a careful study of the Hebrew grammar, it is best to understand this as a simple promise of devotion. It is obvious that this vow was not simply for one instance of tithing, but indicated a practice that would continue throughout Jacob's lifetime. He was not speaking of a crisis so much as a process of giving God the tenth. Further, in this instance there was no priest such as Melchizedek mentioned as the recipient of the tithe. This was an act of direct worship to God, and tithe was considered the giving of a gift to God. This passage constitutes a beautiful example of tithing in the Bible. The practice grows directly out of a fresh encounter with God and the experience of worship related to that encounter. There is not even a hint of legalism in the episode. The commitment is one of a natural, spontaneous desire to honor God with that portion of substance commonly given to the gods of the ancient world.

THE TITHE IN THE MOSAIC LAW

As was the case with earlier sacrifices, the Mosaic Law enfolded, amplified, and codified the practice of tithing. That there appear to be three tithes mentioned in the law is beyond question. Whether these tithes were observed consecutively, concurrently, or one was substituted for another in certain years has been a matter of debate. Those who hold to the documentary theory of the Pentateuch usually conclude that there was one tithe with different interpretations by the various authors. Those who maintain the Mosaic authorship of the Pentateuch see three tithes, although some might have been practiced concurrently or substituted.

The First Tithe: The Lord's and the Levites'

The first tithe is described in Lev. 27:30-33 and expanded in application in Num. 18:21-32. Leviticus opens with the discussion of redemption by a substitute and ends with the declaration that the tithe is holy to God. The subject of the tithe is everything produced by the land, the herd, and the flock. One-tenth of all fruit, grain, calves, and lambs were to be acknowledged as holy. It was not a matter of giving to Yahweh something which belonged to the farmer or shepherd. Rather, the tithe was an acknowledgment that every tenth part already belonged to God. The tithe was an acknowledgment of the fundamental Old Testament principle that God owns the Earth and everything in it. A man could redeem the tithe of the field by paying 20 percent more than the tithe was worth in kind. The tithe of the flock, however, could not be so exchanged: both the beast and the money were considered holy. In giving from the flock, the shepherd could not choose which animals to give.

Maimonides explained that the shepherd would make an enclosure with a gate small enough for only one lamb to leave at a time. The dams would be placed outside the enclosure. As the lambs heard the bleating of the dams they would leave one at a time. As they left, they would pass under the rod of the shepherd. He would mark every tenth one with a red mark, indicating it was holy to God. An expansion of the first tithe occurs in Num. 18:21-32. The recipients of the tithe were to be the tribe of Levi. In the division of the land, these persons devoted to the service of God had received no tribal territory. In light of their service to God at the sanctuary and the absence of their own ancestral lands, the other tribes were to give the tenth for their maintenance. In turn, the Levites were to tithe a tenth of the tithe they received to the priestly family, Aaron and his descendants.

Several principles emerge from these accounts. The tithe already belongs to God. In the tithe we give God but God's own, the minimum any ancient people gave. That tithe comes from all the increase of productivity, both the field and the flock. No area was to be exempt or set aside in the economy which did not belong to God. It is appropriate that the tithe be used for the support of the ministry. Just as Abraham had supported the ministry of Melchizedek with his tithes, so the Mosaic system provided support for the vocational ministry through the giving of tithes. Further, the vocational ministry itself is not exempt from paying the tithe. As already mentioned, the Levites tithed a tenth of the tithe given to them. Thus, there should be no embarrassment on the part of the vocational worker that his or her family is provided for by those they serve (Num. 18:31-32).

The Second Tithe: The Festival Tithe

Deut. 12:5-19 and 14:22-27 proclaim the festival tithe. In order to centralize and regularize the worship of Israel, great emphasis rested upon the place at which this tithe was to be given. It was to be at the central shrine of the nation, at religious headquarters. This would have been first at Shiloh where the ark was parked and later at Jerusalem. The purpose of the festival tithe was vastly different from that of the Lord's tithe. The festival tithe was to be brought to the religious center and eaten there in a celebrative feast marked by an expression of religious joy. The sons, daughters, male and female servants, and the Levites were to partake of the feast eaten in the presence of the Lord. There was a practical reason behind this festival tithe. The Hebrews were to gather together at the national shrine for a week each at Passover and the Feast of Booths, as well as for a shorter time at the Feast of Weeks (Deut. 16:3, 13, 16). The opportunity to partake of the tithe at these festivals both enabled and ensured the participation of the nation at these significant times.

There was a relative discretion in this tithe. If the worshiper lived at too great a distance from the central shrine to take gifts in kind, he could convert them into money. At the place of central worship he could convert the money into whatever he wanted to eat at the feast, including oxen, sheep, wine, or strong drink (Deut. 14:26). This was all to be done in a spirit of rejoicing. Behind this is the abiding principle that stewardship is a shared experience in the worshiping community. Just as giving brings the giver into vital contact with God, so it also brings the giver into fellowship with others. The joy of the shared meal at the festival tithe demonstrates a giving that was no mere legalistic enterprise to be endured. There is a *koinonia* in the giving community brought together in the act of sharing God's creation and goodness.

Often commentators make the distinction between moral and ceremonial law. Some would understand that the Lord's tithe belongs to timeless moral law and the festival tithe belongs to ceremonial law that passed away with the Christian dispensation. This might indeed be the case, but certain principles abide from the festival tithe. There is a rightness of emphasis about the place where the worshiper brings his or her gifts. In the religious pluralism of modern life, there are countless appeals to spread giving over a great sphere of worthy churches, missions, and charities. Surely, it is an abiding principle that the giver should give the gift at the primary place of worship. Further, it abides that giving should be done in a spirit of joy and celebration. Such celebrative spirit in giving has become the rare exception rather than the norm in the churches' giving.

The Third Tithe: The Charitable Tithe

It rests beyond the scope of this investigation to reproduce the historical debate as to whether or not this third tithe replaces the celebrative tithe in the third and sixth years of the sabbatical cycle. Even if it could be proved so, it would not relieve the Christian of serious consideration that giving "above and beyond" the tithe for the relief of the poor is part of every believer's responsibility to God. The third tithe is described in Deut. 14:28-29 and 26:12-15. This tithe was to be given at the end of every three years. The worshiper was to lay this tithe up within his or her own gates. The Levite, stranger, fatherless, and the widow were to access this bounty and eat to the point of satisfaction. For the stranger without land of his or her own this could mean freedom from starvation. There were no community chests or shelters for orphans. Widows had no social security program. Provision for the needs of the weak and poor rested totally in the hands of the worshiper who remembered them for God's sake. The continued blessing of God on the life of the giver depended on this faithfulness to the needy (Deut. 15:4-5). Stewardship which honors God takes into the account the needs of those around the giver.

That the Mosaic Law called for as much as three tithes should cause the modern Christian to reflect. It appears that in the divine economy the tithe has always been the point of departure, not the end of the process. That giving a tenth of the gross lays more burden on the poorer person than the richer is obvious. To give one-tenth of a $20,000 income changes personal lifestyle far more than giving one-tenth of a $200,000 income. The tithe should never be seen as fulfilling all responsibility an affluent person has toward God or those in need around him or her.

Later References to the Tithe

After the references to the tithe in the Pentateuch, the later Old Testament references to the tithe are found in Amos 4:4, the revival under Hezekiah recorded in 2 Chr. 31:2-19, Neh. 10:37, and Malachi 3.

Amos was an eighth-century BC prophet who prophesied during the reigns of Uzziah of Judah and Jeroboam II of Israel. Much of his message was aimed at the Northern capital city Samaria. Religion had become an empty formalism, while social oppression characterized a society divided between the rich and the poor. Amos 4 begins with a biting indictment of the bourgeoise women who live indolently in Samaria. They are indifferent to the need around them and goad their husbands to bring wine home after work. Amos foresees the days when they will be led through gaps in the broken walls of the conquered and defenseless city like a herd of cows, one following the other. In this context, Amos speaks with a biting sarcasm:

Come to Bethel and transgress,
At Gilgal multiply transgression;
Bring your sacrifices every morning,
Your tithes every three days (Amos 4:4).

At the conclusion of this indictment, Amos taunts Israel for their love of mere ceremony: "For this you love, you children of Israel!" (Amos 4:5). Israel apparently thought they were multiplying offerings at the two shrines of the Northern Kingdom, Bethel and Gilgal. Instead, the prophet taunts them that they were multiplying transgressions by following a punctilious, legalistic giving in the face of rampant social injustice. It is unlikely that they actually brought tithes every three days. This might be a mocking reference to the festival tithe or the tithe to the poor offered every three years. God will not be appeased with a mere outward, formal expression of one-dimensional stewardship. After a scathing rejection of the entire current scheme of sacrifice, God speaks through Amos: "Let justice run down like water, and righteousness like a mighty stream" (Amos 5:24). The Old Testament prophets did not accept tithing as a substitute for concern with social justice or other issues of ethical life. This prepares the way for Jesus' statement condemning those who counted off ten leaves of kitchen spice plants, giving every tenth to God, while neglecting justice, mercy, and faith (Matt. 23:23).

Hezekiah became king at age twenty-five and reigned for twenty-nine years in Jerusalem. He led a religious revival which enjoys the most extensive account of any recorded in biblical history (2 Chr. 29:1 - 31:21). During the latter part of the eighth century BC he reformed the Temple, encouraged the practice of religion, and revitalized the system of offerings. The people brought a tithe of oxen, sheep, and other consecrated things, then continued from the third until the seventh month with such abundance the materials began to pile up in heaps. A series of storerooms had to be built adjacent to the Temple in order to contain the abundance of gifts that came from this renewal of tithing (2 Chr. 31:5-10). This revival of religion evidenced a revival of stewardship. It follows the Old Testament pattern of a renewal in relationship with God issuing in a renewal of stewardship.

Nehemiah treats those events around the third wave of return from Exile in 444 BC. His work centered around rebuilding the fallen walls of Jerusalem. In that culture for the walls of a city to be down indicated that the God of the city could not defend the city. It was a negative reflection on the religion of the people for the walls of their city to be down. After reconstruction of the walls, there was a renewal of the religious life of Jerusalem. Part of this involved the bringing of tithes to the Levites. Rather than bringing the tithes to Jerusalem, the Levites—accompanied by priests—received the tithes in the farming communities outside the city. A tithe of the tithe was to be brought for the sustenance of the priests, the gatekeepers, and the singers at the Temple. Storerooms at the Temple were made available for gifts of grain, new wine, and oil. All of this was to avoid neglect of God's house (Neh. 10:37-39).

Finally, that passage most identified with tithing in the whole canonical record is Mal. 3:8-12. The last of the literary prophets, Malachi, wrote in the postexilic period (ca. 435 BC). His epoch followed the Captivity and Restoration by enough time that the society of renewal was already decayed. Ritualism characterized religion and degeneracy marked the moral life of God's people. As part of his indictment, Malachi pointed to the failure of God's people to render the sacred tenth.

Surely, the piercing question of Mal. 3:8 resounds through the centuries as one of the most resonant: "Will a man rob God?" In talmudic literature, the verb *qabā'* very often means "to take forcibly." The implication clearly stands that Judah had committed grand theft against God by taking that which belongs to God. Behind this rests the Levitical teaching noted above that the tithe already belonged to God. It was *qādōš*, set aside with an energetic, kinetic holiness that circumscribed its use for anything else. The very word used by Malachi, maʿăśēr (tenth) was spoken of by Moses as "holy to the Lord" (Lev. 27:30). Even though the tithes were given to the Levites and through them to the priests, it is God who had been robbed. The result of this robbery was barrenness, sterility, and lack of fecundity in the land. Life had become fruitless because God had been robbed. The "whole" nation had fallen under this curse, not just some of the people. There is a solidarity of robbery, a conspiracy afoot in the land that refuses to give God that which is God's. The reversal of this robbery was to bring the "whole" tithe into the storehouse. This "wholeness" must have referred to a tenth of the field, the flock, and the vineyard—the best and the first from each. The "storehouse" indicated the treasury rooms built at the Temple. Whether or not this indicates "storehouse" tithing in which all gifts are given to the local church has been a matter of heated debate. At least the passage places by principle the burden of proof on giving elsewhere than the local assembly where one worships.

The people are invited to "test" God at just this point. Israel is to examine God's very integrity at the point of blessing the people who return to give God the tithe. To those who so return the tithe, God offers to give such abundant blessing that there will not be room to receive it (Mal. 3:10). This might refer to the inability of humans to store that which God so abundantly gives. Or there might be the irony that God would be so generous that heaven itself would run out of resources to give; God would have to have a respite from giving so generously. Of course, that is laughable and absurd. Either way, the indication is a generosity of such proportions that there is no way to calculate it.

God will respond by rebuking the devourer (Mal. 3:11). A futility enters life when humans rob God of the sacred tenth. When they give God that which is God's, God will so act as to end everything that frustrates and retards the efficiency of human labor. Work will be worth it again. When the people give to God as God intended, the other nations of the Earth will acknowledge that they are "blessed." This is the very word that was used of the impact of Abraham's descendants on the world (Gen. 12:1-3). Hence, the study of the Old Testament has come full circle. The first book of the Old Testament promised that through the offspring of Abraham of Ur the whole planet would be blessed. The last book of the Old Testament ends with a sober reminder that the whole Earth will be blessed when the true descendants of Abraham honor God as stewards.

The New Testament
Expression of Stewardship

Stewardship in the New
Testament can be seen as a continuation of that which God
began in the Old Testament. We can intentionally contrast the
themes of the Old Testament section of this book with its further development in the New Testament. The Creator God of
the Old Testament becomes the Redeemer Christ of the New
Testament. A created heaven and Earth will become a
redeemed heaven and Earth. Created humans become re-created humans. The people of the land become the people of the
Kingdom with a new covenant, a new worship, and a new mission. Thus, the New Testament indeed "fulfills" the old in the
full sense of Jesus' intent (Matt. 5:17). He is the embodiment of
that fulfillment, and He fills the Old Testament meaning to the
brim with God's intention.

CHRIST AS REDEEMER

Since the major axis of the Old Testament doctrine of stewardship is the creation and ownership of God, the major theme of
New Testament stewardship is the Redemption of Christ, the

buying back of that which has been lost to sin. This Redemption plays itself out in the major themes of the Incarnation, Cross, and Resurrection.

The Real Incarnation

"And the Word became flesh and dwelt among us" (John 1:14). No statement of the New Testament has a more profound meaning for stewardship. Indeed, stewardship becomes meaningless if there was not a real Incarnation of God in the advent of Jesus Christ. In Bethlehem, what happened was nothing less than God invading history in the form of the babe of the manger. Behind that tiny, soft, infantile forehead rested the mind of God. Those chubby baby fingers were the fingers of God incarnate. The conception of Jesus Christ was nothing less than an invasion of Mary's womb by the power of God which resulted in the miracle of a virginal conception and birth. In some way, the chromosomes of God intertwined with those of Mary and conceived God incarnate.

When God became flesh, it meant that the eternal and spiritual had entered the temporal and physical. In order to redeem, eternity entered time and spirituality cleaved to the physical in a way theretofore unexampled. When that happened, all time changed into God's redeemed time and all that was physical glowed with the possibility of the spiritual. Incarnation not only enabled but modeled the true sense of stewardship—God invading the material and temporal universe to buy it back.

To reduce this to its most immediate and practical, the only way placing a monetary gift into an offering place is not an audacious act of impertinence on the part of puny humans is the Incarnation. That God could be clothed in the material makes possible our own giving of the material back to God as part of God's redemptive purposes.

One of the first great battles of the church was that of docetic gnosticism. This insidious doctrine taught that there was only an apparent incarnation. Gnosticism was a philosophical system that, among other things, taught the utter impossibility of God relating to the material universe. It was an extension of Greek Platonism in which a "good" spiritual god could never enter "evil" human flesh. This kind of dualism renders the Incarnation impossible. For the docetic gnostics, Jesus only seemed to be human. He was an ephemeral mirage, a floating visage that only seemed to be walking among humans or on water. This kind of absolute idealism gave birth in American religious history to such cults as Christian Science, a radical denial of the reality of physical life, sin, and death (and along with that, of the possibility of real redemption).

For that reason John, the gospel that most emphasizes Jesus' divinity, also most emphasizes His real humanity. He sat down on the curb of the well at Sychar weary from the journey (John 4:6). At the tomb of Lazarus, Jesus "wept" and "groaned" (John 11:35, 38). That is, He felt the full horror of the presence of death as any human would feel. Nothing of this was playacting. God had become flesh, our flesh weary with a journey and grieving at the death of a friend. So eager was John to combat this docetic gnosticism that he even emphasized how the disciples had "handled" Jesus after the Resurrection (1 John 1:1). The Word refers to the same way blind Isaac's hand reached and groped for Esau and Jacob in order to prove their identities.

This embracing of the invasion of the physical by the material finds its ultimate expression in the revelation in which John "saw the holy city, New Jerusalem, coming down out of heaven from God, prepared as a bride adorned for her husband" (Rev. 21:2). The pattern of the eternal order in which all things are to become new is the same downward pattern of the Incarnation of the Christ. The city of God comes down from above into the midst of the renewed physical condition of human beings so that "the tabernacle of God is with men" (Rev. 21:3). The eternal order is not a sweeping of humans into the immaterial dimension of the spiritual, but rather a coming of God to sanctify forever the very real circumstances in which humans have lived—redeemed forever in the eternal order.

In Greek dualism and docetic gnosticism, this is an impossible absurdity. The Greeks expressed it *soma sema*, a play on words which means "the body is a tomb." The goal of such philosophy was a disembodied existence as far as possible from the physical. The amazing, shattering, radical word of the Christian message is just the opposite. God enters into the material world and redeems it in its materiality. Indeed, God takes up and uses the very materiality of that world in God's program of redemption.

Nowhere is this underscored more finally than in the Christian view of the resurrection of the body. This corruptible, dishonored, weak, natural body will be raised; a body not subject to decay, but a glorious, strong, and a spiritual body—a body capable of displaying the life of the Spirit (1 Cor. 15:42-44). We will abide forever in the presence of God with a body that is a glorious continuation of this present physical body. The material will be caught into the spiritual and redeemed. God can enter into the material and use it for divine purposes.

This is the absolute foundation of stewardship: God uses the material for divine purposes. The implication of this lifts up and hallows all of life.

The Incarnation implies that God can enter the human mind and use it. What makes the difference between the mind of a Billy Graham and an Adolf Hitler, two of the twentieth century's titanic figures? What makes the difference between the fiendish mind that blows up a building in Oklahoma or the devout mind that translates the Bible into a tribal language? Incarnation means that God can enter the human mind and make the mind a steward of God's purposes.

The Incarnation means that God can enter the human body and use it. What distinguishes the animal strength of a brutal serial killer from the endurance of a Bill Wallace of China or a Mother Teresa of India? God can enter the body and create a stewardship of physical strength.

The Incarnation means that God can enter the creative arts of humans. What causes the brutish pornographer to differ from Michelangelo? What causes the vulgar rap group to be different from Handel? The human creative capacity is entered and redeemed by God for God's use. God creates a stewardship of art. Wherever one chooses to touch human life, the Incarnation makes possible the stewardship of that life for the purposes of God. If God had not entered time and space in the Incarnation of Jesus Christ, such stewardship would be impossible. We would be a planet of mud-bound semi-apes, never escaping the downward drag of spiritual gravity or the inertia of our own sloth. When God touched the material world at Bethlehem, it set loose in human history the powerful force of God-become-flesh. From that time forward, every place and every time became the locus and moment for the possibility of stewardship. We are now trustees of a new humanity which God entered and redeemed. That has rent the veil and made the entire world the holy of holies.

In his famous treatise *Cur Deus Homo?* Anselm asked the question, "Why God Man?" He argued that the Incarnation was necessary for the Atonement. Indeed, it was. But we can take that a step further. The Incarnation was necessary for any real, authentic understanding of stewardship. If God is such a monad—the Moslem Allâh—that God cannot come into real contact with humanity by Incarnation, then God cannot in reality redeem the material aspects of humankind's own existence, no less the environment around it. The Incarnation means that God has touched and sanctified the material world by entering into that world. There is nothing which in and of itself cannot be taken up into the purposes of God. Even as Adam was steward in the Garden and failed in that stewardship, now the last Adam enters the desert and turns it into the place of stewardship for the purposes of God. In that sense, the Bible is a place of three gardens.

- In the first garden—Eden—humans lost the opportunity to be the steward God intended them to be.
- In the second garden—Gesthemane—the incarnate Son of God won back that stewardship of God's purposes.
- In the final garden, the New Jerusalem of Revelation 21-22, humankind is once again in a garden with a beautiful river lined by trees for the healing of the nations. It is a fulfillment of God's intention for humans as stewards and servants in that which God had created.

The Crucial Cross

The center of the Christian message in the Western church has always been the Cross of Christ. Even though Eastern Orthodoxy seems to emphasize the Incarnation over the Cross, the church as we know it places the Cross in the center of God's mighty act in the coming of the Christ. Since that is so, the Cross must also have profound implications for stewardship in the shadow of that Cross.

A crucial question about the Cross is that of its necessity. Was it necessary for what God wishes to do in the world that the incarnate Christ should die on the Cross? The New Testament does not so much explain as assume the necessity of the Cross. The so-called Passion Sayings of Jesus pictured the Cross as a great moral necessity. Immediately after the Great Confession "Jesus began to show to His disciples that He must go to Jerusalem, and suffer many things from the elders and chief priests and scribes, and be killed, and be raised the third day" (Matt. 16:21). In this verse we find the use of the Greek particle *dei* as an indication of necessity. It is a technical term which implies the absolute moral necessity that Christ die on the Cross. The Cross was not an accident or a mere fluke of history. Nor was the Cross the impulsive act of a would-be martyr. In God's intention for the planet, the Cross was a necessity.

Why is the Cross necessary?—because of human sin. The God of the Bible is a God of moral earnestness. God is not a benevolent super Santa Claus who simply winks at human sin and error. The nature of God requires that something be done about sin in order to forgive sin. The Cross must also be seen over-against God's purpose to save. The Greek *sozo* refers to God's desire to make humans whole, to heal them in every dimension of life.

In regard to stewardship, the Cross must be seen in its effect on humankind's failure to be stewards. If Christ died for sin, He certainly died for those sins in which humans fail to be the stewards or trustees God intended them to be. If we are stewards of our own bodies, families, relations, material possessions, and world, then the Cross has profound implications for each. On the Cross, Christ bought our very bodies for His own purposes: "For you were bought at a price; therefore glorify God in your body and in your spirit, which are God's" (1 Cor. 6:20). In a real sense, the most fundamental possession of a person—the very body the person inhabits—was bought, purchased, and redeemed at the Cross. This purchase of the human body and spirit at the Cross constitutes a fundamental of Christian stewardship. Just as God owns me by virtue of creation, God has bought me back in the Redemption of the Cross. Thus, I am doubly a steward, by creation and by redemption.

Consider the implications of the Cross for stewardship according to the varied emphases that gather around the Cross:

The Cross as a Revelation of Love. "God demonstrates His own love toward us, in that while we were still sinners, Christ died for us" (Rom. 5:8). Whereas the Greek and pagan gods were angry deities, the Father of the Lord Jesus demonstrated God's love in the Cross. Christ died to demonstrate the love of God to us. Christ did not just die to propitiate the wrath of God. He died first to demonstrate the love that already rested in God. Stewardship under the Cross is a stewardship that both demonstrates that love and motivates us to act under the stimulus of that love. If Christ kept faith with the stewardship of His redemptive mission because of love, then our stewardship must be activated by that kind of love that flows from the Cross.

One urban minister preached a sermon entitled "*A Cross in My Pocket.*" He asked the congregation to consider the keychain in their pockets or purses. On it were the symbols of their stewardship in life. The house key represented their homes; the car key represented their mobility; the office key represented their vocation; the safety deposit key represented their material security. Then the preacher conspicuously placed a small metal cross on the keychain in the midst of those keys. At the conclusion of the service, he passed out little crosses to be placed on the keychains of the entire congregation. He called for them to consider the implications of the Cross for every facet of life represented by the keys. This gave a poignant reminder of the centrality of the Cross in the stewardships of home life, work life, and material life.

If Christians could live with the sense of the Cross in their pockets, at their desks, in their checkbooks, or covering the dial of their watches, it could radically affect our view of the stewardship of time, talent, and treasure.

The Cross as a Sacrifice. Paul deliberately relates the death of Christ to the Old Testament view of sacrifice. By calling Christ the *hilasterion* (place of atonement, Rom. 3:25), Paul makes a definite allusion to the Old Testament system of sacrifice described in chapter 2. Christ's death is "an offering and a sacrifice to God" (Eph. 5:2). This is a further reflection of the sacrificial system of the Old Testament. All references to redemption through the blood of Christ of course point to that death as a sacrifice (Eph. 1:7).

Central to any view of stewardship must be the concept of sacrifice. Sacrifice means giving up something I love for something I love and cherish more. Sacrifice means giving something

81

which changes my lifestyle. The ultimate picture of sacrifice was the giving of Christ's life. His life was something of infinite value, a perfectly sinless life never out of fellowship with God. Yet He gave up that life for God's purposes.

The New Testament makes it clear that the Cross is something which the Christian must share. We renounce all, take up our cross, and follow Him (Mark 8:34ff). We are to live as those who constantly carry with us the symbol of death to ourselves. This self-denial is not so much a denial of certain things or items as it is a standing apart from ourselves. We say of ourselves: "I do not know this man, this woman." This has the most profound significance for stewardship. There would be no "stewardship drives" if each individual Christian understood all of life as a bearing of the Cross of Christ. How could one withhold any dimension of stewardship if one understands life as a cross-bearing discipleship. The Christian shares the Cross in a life of self-denial. This is not meaningless suffering for suffering's sake. To live as a steward under the Cross is to lose self in the service of Christ.

The Cross as Vicarious. The death of Christ was in a real way "for us" (Rom. 5:8; 8:32). The death of Christ was not just another of the billions of deaths that have happened on planet Earth. He became a "curse" for us (Gal. 3:13). Jesus Christ became in the most profound sense "the Man for others." As an extension of this, the life of consistent stewardship becomes a vicarious life, a life lived for others.

One of the dividing lines of human life and personality is that line which determines whether or not a person consumes life entirely for selfish purposes or becomes a person for others. In the vicarious death of Christ we see the stewardship of life for others embodied in the Cross.

The Cross as Redemption. There are two groups of words in the New Testament that emphasize the death of Christ as a redemption. Some of those words relate to the stem *lutron* and others relate to the verb *agarazo*. In Greek, the former is used of the price paid to redeem something pawned, money paid to redeem prisoners of war, or money paid to purchase the freedom of a slave. The latter word more simply means to purchase or to pay a price. "You are not your own. For you were bought at a price" (1 Cor. 6:19-20). In a profound sense, the death of Christ caused a change in ownership. The believer has been purchased by God and in that light is the possession of God, purchased by the blood of Christ.

That we belong to God means that we are the servants, and stewards, of the One who bought us. If we are not our own, then nothing about us is our own. Our bodies, time, energy, jobs, homes, education, and networks all belong to God. We operate under new ownership. Redemption is the New Testament corollary of Old Testament creation. Since God owns us by reason of creation, God has purchased what God already owned in the redemptive act of Christ. This creates a double motive for faithfulness in stewardship.

The Cross as Triumph over Evil Powers. "Having disarmed principalities and powers, He made a public spectacle of them, triumphing over them in it" (Col. 2:15). In the cosmic victory of the Cross, Christ in some mysterious way stripped or disarmed those cosmic powers that hold humans in bondage. This had implications far beyond the salvation of the individual human from sin. Whatever there is inside and outside of humans that degrades, demeans, imprisons, tortures, perverts, or debases them has been dealt with by the death of Christ. In that whole event of Christ's passion which began with His torture, led through His Cross, His tomb, His Resurrection, and finally His triumphant Ascension, humans and ultimately their environment were freed from the tyranny of the hostile and malignant spiritual powers that enslave.

In days when news magazines devote cover stories to the reality and source of evil, late-twentieth-century philosophy has come to again ponder the imponderable presence of evil. It is so pervasive and persistent there must be behind it a personal life of its own. Christianity answers that in the Passion. Jesus began the defeat of evil which will be complete at His Second Advent.

Since this is so, stewardship is vaulted into an even more exalted plane. When you use time, talent, and resources to forward the redemptive plan of Christ, you are participating in His ongoing campaign to defang every serpent that poisons life in time and eternity. Those hours given in His service and those dollars given in His work translate into part of the cosmic victory that began on the Cross. When a Christian missionary goes to India, a Christian college educates young people in the knowledge of God, a Christian hospital practices healing, a Christian prison ministry brings hope to the incarcerated, the liberating campaign begun on the Cross thrusts itself forward in time.

The Validating Resurrection

The Resurrection of Jesus Christ is not defended but rather assumed by the New Testament. If Jesus were not raised from the dead, one of several things must have happened:
- Jesus deceived the Apostles and beyond that the whole human race. That the Jesus of the Gospels could conceivably do such a thing contradicts all reason.

- Jesus and the Apostles entered into a pact to deceive the human race. That would mean while Peter preached at Pentecost, Jesus was somewhere hiding, laughing up His sleeve so to speak, at the scam perpetrated on the human race. This is unthinkable in the face of the record of Jesus' teaching.
- The Apostles knew that Jesus was dead but entered into a conspiracy to deceive the human race by stating that Jesus rose when they knew He did not. As history has noted, the Watergate Conspiracy did not last but for a few days. John Dean bolted and became "state's evidence" after a short time. If the Apostles lied about the Resurrection of Jesus, they entered into a lifelong conspiracy for which all but one of them died. That is unlikely.
- The Jews or Romans hid the body of Jesus. This is the most unlikely theory of all. If they had done so, all they had to do when Christianity exploded at Pentecost and created civil disobedience in Jerusalem was to produce the body of Jesus.

This chapter is not a treatise on apologetics to defend the Resurrection. Yet the above is a reminder that the Resurrection rests not only on scriptural but also rational bases. How does the Resurrection relate to stewardship?

The Endorsement of the Cross

According to Paul in Rom. 1:4, Jesus was "declared to be the Son of God with power according to the Spirit of holiness, by the resurrection from the dead." The Resurrection validated, endorsed, and authenticated all that Jesus said and did. The Resurrection was God's great "Yes" to the life, work, and words of Jesus. Those words included Jesus' teaching about stewardship. It has often been noted that one of every six verses in the Gospels treat some aspect of stewardship. The Resurrection of Jesus included God's validation of Jesus' teaching, including His teaching about stewardship. Had Jesus remained in the cold, unrelaxed embrace of death, there would have been no certainty about the truth of His teachings. The Resurrection was a vindication of everything Jesus said and did, including all He said about the stewardship of life. His viewpoint on the trusteeship of time, talent, and treasure emerged triumphant in the Resurrection. When those eyes closed in death opened again, that breath abated in death breathed again, and those feet stilled in death walked again, it was the heavenly ratification of Jesus' viewpoint on life as a steward of God.

But most specifically, the Resurrection was God's vindication of Jesus' death on the Cross. It was previously noted that the Cross as Redemption implies a profound view of stewardship as sacrifice and a vicarious view of life for others. How do we know that Jesus' view of life as expressed in the Cross squares with ultimate reality? We know it only by the Resurrection.

The Resurrection as a Continuation of Life in the World

If humans die and decompose into nothingness, no act in the world has any abiding significance for eternity. Certainly, this is true of the death of Jesus Christ. To the extent that His resurrection life on Earth demonstrates the life to come for all believers, it demonstrates the significant continuity of what we are in this world with the life to come. The resurrection body of Jesus showed both a continuity and a discontinuity with the life He had shared in the world.

The Resurrection of Jesus was a continuity with the life He shared in the world. When Jesus appeared to His disciples, He took pains to demonstrate that He was the same Jesus, not another entity: "Behold My hands and My feet, that it is I Myself. Handle Me and see, for a spirit does not have flesh and bones as you see I have" (Luke 24:39). The implication of this continuity for stewardship deserves more attention than it has been given.

First, we are stewards of our own body. We are not our own; we have been bought through the sacrifice of Jesus and further belong to God by reason of creation. We are twice-owned by God. In some mysterious way, we will take that body in continuity into the world to come. Paul makes this clear in 1 Cor. 15:35-49. The body of which we were trustee will be renewed with continuity in the life everlasting. This vests what we do in this world with the deepest significance. Just as scientists say that no radio transmission is ever totally lost, but continues in ever-decreasing power into the vastness of space, so no act in the body is ever completely lost in time and eternity. That we will continue in another edition of the same body hallows all life in the body with a significance beyond the grave. What we do with time, talents, and treasure is done "in the body." The body is the medium or vehicle of stewardship: "For we must all appear before the judgment seat of Christ, that each one may receive the things done in the body, according to what he has done, whether good or bad" (2 Cor. 5:10).

The Resurrection vests temporal or corporeal life with an eternal significance. Jesus did not disappear into a platonic, disembodied state of spirit. He emerged with a resurrection body. This underscores the value of the temporal life in light of the eternal life. What is done on Earth will have continuity with what happens beyond Earth.

Further, it is the resurrection life of Christ within us that cuts the nerve of covetousness and makes possible a life of stewardship, a life for God and others: "For if when we were enemies we were reconciled to God through the death of His Son, much more, having been reconciled, we shall be saved by His life" (Rom. 5:10). The Christian life is possible only because a new principle of life has entered into our earthly, temporal life. Major Ian Thomas and the Keswick movement has called this "the saving life of Christ." When the resurrected life of Christ enters the inherently selfish life of a human, a new principle overcomes the downward drag of selfishness. This is the expulsive power of a new affection. Just as a thrifty young man will suddenly spend money lavishly on the new love of his life, the Christian invaded by the resurrection life of Christ begins to operate out of a new principle, one that expels that grasp of greed and freely gives because of the new life that has entered.

HEAVEN AND EARTH AS REDEMPTION

Just as we can contrast God as Creator with Christ as Redeemer, we might also compare the Old Testament creation of Heaven and Earth with the New Testament redemption of Heaven and Earth. If God as Creator expresses ownership and Earth as creation expresses stewardship, Christ as Redeemer expressed a double ownership and Earth as re-creation expresses a more profound stewardship. The destiny of this planet is ultimate redemption through the cosmic renewal in Jesus Christ. As will be demonstrated in chapter 7, the cosmic context clamors for attention in today's world.

The Cry of Creation

That there is chaos and disorder in creation can be recognized by mere empirical observation. In Rom. 8:19, Paul moves beyond speculation to a profound revelation. The total of all creation—animate and inanimate—joins together in a great cosmic groan for something better. Whether brute beasts on the great plains of Africa or earthquakes in Kobe, Japan, there is in nature a great cacophonous call for redemption, a return to Eden. Further, this does not consist of a mere passive intent on the part of nature. Paul uses a compound Greek verb that indicates nature stretching its neck and craning forward with the intensity of a runner reaching the finish line with the expectancy that God will intervene redemptively.

This cry of creation calls for the stewardship of Christians now. There is a passive and pessimistic view of the stewardship of the planet in which believers are mere observers of the disintegration until the final intervention of Christ. This temporal fatalism sees the Christian role as evangelism of souls only until the final intervention of God. To this the biblical Christian must object. This passive view is not only an abdication of the mandate for dominion in Genesis but a cancellation of our destiny as stewards of God's creation today waiting for its full redemption tomorrow. In this regard, we are not just waiting on God but also working with God.

The Consummation of Creation

As the millennium hastens toward the year 2000, thoughts will accelerate toward the end of the world. Will it end in a great explosion of the sun that incinerates all life? Will it end in a great viral plague that, like Dustin Hoffman's movie *Outbreak*, decimates the planet with an Ebola-like virus? Will history end as a battlefield of corpses in a worldwide Bosnia-like war? Paul proclaims that the last chapter of cosmic re-creation will begin with "the revealing of the sons of God" (Rom. 8:19b). Believers are now in the world incognito. The Christian in one house looks undramatically like his pagan, secular neighbor in the next house. But on the day of Christ's final Advent, Christians will suddenly be revealed for what they are. In what Paul calls an *atomōs* (1 Cor. 15:52), the least divisible amount of time, there will be a sudden transformation of our weak and dissolving bodies into a body like that of the risen Lord. Simultaneously radiating out in some unknown spiritual signal, some mysterious message will be sent to all creation that the time has come for the Final Transformation of all things. In some way beyond all present knowledge, the big change in Christians will signal the final change in the cosmos.

The implications of this for stewardship are enormous. Not only in this life but in the life to come there is a vital connection between Christians and their environment. What we effect in time and life with our stewardship will resonate out into the cosmos in the great final change. We must take seriously our stewardship of the world now for we are participants with God in what God will do then.

We shall be the first to be changed. God will not give preference to other animals or inorganic creation over us. That would be to change the playing field and leave the same team on it. God will first change us to be like Christ. Only then will creation reverberate with change. In the earliest days of Morse code, messages were carried on two wires spanning the continent. Sometimes the oscillation of one wire would cause the other to vibrate, making it carry the same message. In the final day, those changes in Christians will somehow vibrate in the remainder of creation, and all will be renewed. Our stewardship today is proleptic of that stewardship tomorrow.

The Crisis of Creation

Is the chaos of creation an absurdity like a random confluence of atoms that never got organized? No. God subjected creation to the futility under which it now groans. That state of the universe is because of "Him Who subjected it" (Rom. 8:20a-23). Creation is no bobsled hurling down an endless course. The sonorous mandate of Gen. 3:17-19 is nothing less than the sovereign statement of God: "cursed is the ground for your sake." When the first pair failed in their stewardship of the Garden, the result was a curse on the means of their livelihood. Work became toil.

Paul called the chaotic situation of the natural world "futility." The Greek word *mataiotes* refers to that which does not reach its goal. Because of human lack of accountability to the image of God within and the stewardship of life without, creation has been retarded from reaching the goal God intended. One can see this in the tidal wave, the hurricane, the tornado, the mudslide, or the earthquake. In some ineffable way, these aberrations of nature are connected with the failure of human stewardship as begun in Eden and continuing to this day. C. E. B. Cranfield states the dilemma poignantly:

> We may think of the whole magnificent theatre of the universe together with all its splendid properties and all the chorus of subhuman life, created to glorify God but unable to do so fully, so long as man the chief actor in the drama of God's praise fails to contribute his rational part.[1]

Every discord in creation can be traced to Brunner's "man in revolt." The fact that on this planet Earth—twenty-five thousand miles in circumference, an infinitesimal speck in the immensity of the universe—a race of rebels mutinied against God has in some way wreaked havoc on creation. Why would

God permit pieces of human protoplasm on a tiny planet to inter-ject discord into the flawless praises of God's creation? Redeemed humanity is the very purpose of God's creation. The universe itself cannot be stabilized until those women and men who carry the *imago dei*, the very image of God, experience their own redemption. In other words, when the human race recovers its appropriate stewardship within the dominion God intended, the cosmic universe will reverberate with that restoration.

Every sensate human lives with a sense of angst, primeval dread, that something in creation has warped the entire inten-tion of God. Even thunder can evoke the feeling of something dreadfully obscure. Donald Tuzin of the University of California at San Diego related that sounds caused by certain large drums, bells, gongs, and even chanting have a mysterious quality that affects us beyond the sound itself. It is not so much what can be heard as what cannot be heard. These sounds have frequencies below conscious human perception, below 20 hertz. While these sounds remain inaudible to people, the vibrations do affect the temporal lobe, a part of the brain that's vital to both hearing and memory processing. The listener is left with the perception that something mysterious, beyond perception and understanding, is stirring.[2]

The 1960s produced the slang expression "bad vibes" and "good vibes." Indeed, the universe itself "groans" as well as Christians who "groan within ourselves." There is out there some subliminal, mysterious sighing of the spheres, a grand groaning of cosmic proportions. In the same sense that the ancient Hebrew knew that something disruptive was set in motion when he failed to render to Yahweh the holy tithe of the land, modern people know that something contradicts reason and revelation in the disposition of human resources today. Part of the cosmic renewal anticipated by Romans 8 will be a return to human stewardship of animate and inanimate creation. Stewardship of time, talent, and treasure today anticipates that time when what Christians administer as stewards today will one day be perfected in the Second Advent of Christ and the great *apokatastasis*.

Humans as Re-Creation

The New Testament counterpart to the Old Testament doctrine of humans as creation is the New Testament view of Christians as re-creation. In Christ, God has begun to restore the *imago dei*. "If anyone is in Christ, he is a new creation; old things have passed away; behold, all things have become new" (2 Cor. 5:17). Normally, this verse is applied to the spiritual and moral renewal of the individual through the regenerating power of Christ. The verse, however, refers to more than that. In the coming of Christ a new age has dawned. In Christ there is deliverance from the present evil age (Gal. 1:4). Christians are under no bondage to be conformed to the old age (Rom. 12:2). God has brought about a new creation and we walk through it in the display of good works (Eph. 2:10). Most specifically, the new life in Christ is the putting on of a new humanity "which is being renewed in knowledge after the image of its Creator (Col. 3:9-10). If the *imago dei* is being restored in the new aeon of Christ, it means a new understanding, motive, and practice of stewardship.

The new creation in Christ must have a new understanding of stewardship. The Old Testament system of gifts and sacrifices embraced a material part of life. It tutored the Hebrews in the elements of beginning stewardship. Yet the Christian cannot be satisfied as part of the new creation to limit stewardship to sporadic episodes of giving at the appointed times and places. Since a new age has begun with the victory of Christ, the stage of stewardship is enlarged to all of life. This is a natural progression from seeing stewardship as a matter of episodes designated by the law of God.

There must now be a new motive and energy for steward-ship. If the Old Testament giving was based on the Exodus, the New Testament giving rests on the Cross and the Resurrection. As both motive and energy, these realities of the new age trans-form stewardship of time, talent, and treasure. A central cate-gory of the New Testament for re-created humanity is the phrase "in Christ." This remarkable phrase coins a new idiom in language. No one in the ancient world was said to be "in Caesar" or "in Alexander." The believers lived out of the expe-rience of a reality that placed Christ in them and them in Christ. As the bird lives in the air and must have the air to live, as the fish lives in water and must have the water to live, so the believer lives in Christ. The believer is in Christ and Christ is in the believer. We can understand this better when we know that the ancient peoples could understand spiritual life as a fine invisible matter that could interpenetrate all visible forms of matter. In their view, to be "in Christ" was to be interpenetrat-ed with a new, personal life force.

Ladd suggests that this can best be understood in contrast to the expression "in Adam."[3] Paul sees Adam and Christ as the heads of two races living simultaneously on this planet. The race of Adam is caught up in the sin-death principle, living according to the flesh. The race of Christ lives out of the victory of its Lord, living according to the Spirit. All humans belong to one or the other of the races. Adam for-feited his stewardship in Eden. He had been given full rights as a tenant for an absentee Lord of the Garden. After the expulsion from Eden, Adam's race lived with the consequences of that discarded stewardship.

Thomas Cole (1801–1848) was a self-taught landscape artist who emigrated from England to America. In 1828 he painted two imaginary landscapes, The Garden of Eden and the Expulsion from the Garden of Eden. They hung together side by side for the first time since 1829 in 1995 at the Kimbell Art Museum in Fort Worth, Texas. Drawing on images from the Bible and John Milton, Cole powerfully presents our present predicament. In the Garden of Eden, Adam and Eve stand as two figures dwarfed by an Earth at peace with itself. In the foreground, the primordial springs reveal gigantic precious stones. In the middle, animal and plant life reveal a world in perfect harmony. In the far background, a snowy mountain towers over an ever-running Edenic river. It is creation as God intended it to be.

Hanging next to this, however, is the painting Expulsion from Eden. Once again, Adam and Eve are dwarfed. This time they are crossing the "bridge of fear" from Eden to the blasted world outside its gates. Cole represented this world as volcanic eruption over the weird form of blasted, grotesque, and twisted trees. A hungry jackal feasts on the lifeless, gray form of a fawn. Conversely, in the painting of Eden the fawn plays in the emerald grass of the Garden. Yet in the Expulsion, the viewer can still see Eden inside the gates, forever green and peaceful, just beyond the reach or return of human life. Life outside of Eden reflects life "in Adam." Ultimately, what God intended in Eden will be consummated "in Christ."

In the interpretation of Old Testament stewardship above, the human stewardship rooted in Genesis 1-3 was examined in detail. The creation of Adam, the *imago dei*, and the revolt against that accountable stewardship to God framed the picture of life in Adam. Now life in Christ restores that possibility, a new energy for the re-creation of God's original intention. We know the love of God in Christ Jesus (Rom 8:39), service in Christ (Phil. 2:5), and contentment in every kind of human context in Christ (Phil. 4:13). All of life is conducted in Christ (1 Cor. 4:17). This new reality of life in Christ yields the potential of stewardship motivated by the love of God, time and talent given in Christ, and a context of stewardship growing out of the contentment with all circumstances found in Christ. With the motive of love, the expression of service, the context of contentment, and the energy of the risen Christ enabling the re-creation of stewardship, the concept of steward is lifted to another altitude of spirituality.

Life in the new creation overcomes the downward drag of the flesh. It rests beyond the scope of this brief theological overview to rehearse the vast amount of material on *sarx*, the flesh. Covetousness, greed, and self-absorption root in the flesh. Flesh, in the Pauline sense, is all humans are, apart from the life of Christ. Flesh is the bridgehead of sin in human life. Flesh is an all-pervasive drag on spiritual life, a gravity that pulls down the spiritual life. Just as flesh is the enemy of all spiritual life, it is the locus of enmity to a life of stewardship. Flesh grasps, covets, centers life in the ego, and clasps time, talent, and treasure in its octopus grip. Flesh is like Medusa of Greek mythology—when you cut off one head, it only grows more. There is not escape from flesh except life in the Spirit.

Paul can exult "You are not in the flesh, but in the Spirit" (Rom. 8:9). The flesh is dead because it has been crucified (Gal.

5:24). Although Paul is in the world, he no longer lives in the world (Gal. 6:14). Because of the reality of life in Christ, the world is dead to Paul and Paul to the world. The believer has died to the elements of the world (Col. 2:20). Life in the world is at enmity with life as a steward. The world considers that individuals belong to themselves, answer to themselves, and live to maintain themselves. Life in the world is life in the flesh. This undercuts the possibility of life as a total stewardship. When the life of the Spirit nullifies and renders inoperative life in the flesh, it becomes possible to be a total steward. The flesh-world axis militates against a worldview of stewardship. The *kosmos* is the world as organized against God. It is animated by the *Zeitgeist*, the spirit of the age which always expresses hostility to God and the values of God's people. So strong is the flesh-world combination that it effectively poisons any approach to stewardship. Only life in Christ through the Spirit provides the thrust to lift the believer above the downward drag of the flesh-world.

The other aspect of re-creation in the new aeon is life in the Spirit. The investigation of Paul's view about the risen Christ as he relates to the Holy Spirit fills volumes. Suffice it to say that the Spirit is the way Christ works in the new aeon. Only the Spirit enables us to understand what God is doing in Christ (1 Cor. 2:6-13). The Spirit imparts faith (2 Cor. 4:13). The Spirit creates a sense of sonship (Rom. 8:15-16) and creates direct access to the Father (Eph. 3:16-17). The Spirit helps in prayer (Rom. 8:26) and enables believers to grasp the greatness of God's love (Eph. 3:16-17). The Spirit also enables believers to offer true worship to God: "For we are the circumcision, who worship God in the Spirit [in the Spirit of God], rejoice in Christ Jesus, and have no confidence in the flesh" (Phil. 3:3). As we discovered in the investigation of the Old Testament, biblically, the relationship between worship and stewardship cannot be dissolved. Since the new aeon brings a new worship "in the Spirit," there is a new impetus for stewardship. It no longer belongs to one place (the Temple) at specific times (the Levitical offering system) in strictly defined categories of animal, cereal, or liquid offerings.

Peter expanded on this new worship in 1 Pet. 2:5. "You also as living stones, are being built up a spiritual house, a holy priesthood, to offer up spiritual sacrifices acceptable to God through Jesus Christ." Here Peter presents a new temple, priesthood, and system of sacrifices. Believers constitute a new temple of "living stones." The lifeless, inanimate massive blocks of the Herodian Temple disappear. They are replaced with the believers of each age and all ages. The Old Testament's male-only adult priesthood is preempted by a priesthood of all believers of all genders and ages. Most significantly, these priests offer new *pneumatikas thusias*, spiritual sacrifices. What could Peter mean by these new sacrifices? His fellow Hebrew Christian author writes in Heb. 13:15-16:

> Therefore by Him let us continually offer the sacrifice of praise to God, that is, the fruit of our lips, giving thanks to His name. But do not forget to do good and to share, for with such sacrifices God is well pleased.

Here is the agenda for the sacrifice by God's new people. Sacrifice begins in the inward dimension of praise. From the center of the believer's personality comes the expression of value toward God. That praise emerges vocally and expresses itself in audible thanks. That in turn expresses itself concretely in "doing good" and in equally concrete acts of *koinonia*. Here the author uses the word for fellowship or intimate joint participation in the tangible sense "to communicate" (AV, RV), meaning to give to the needs of others. This places stewardship on a grounds far away from any legalistic impulse or intention to manipulate God for a reciprocal blessing. Here indeed all of life becomes a temple, every act the act of a priest, and each moment a shining possibility of stewardship. That this includes all that is generally intended by stewardship of material resources is significant, but almost an afterthought. If every dimension of life is lifted up to God as a spiritual sacrifice, the monetary aspect of giving will follow as naturally as the opening of a rose in the warm light of spring. In this regard, much teaching on stewardship is wide of the mark. When giving is singled out as some exceptional aspect of Christian living apart from the larger context of the new life in Christ, it is devoid of its larger motivation and meaning. The motivation of New Testament giving should be the larger context of praise, thanksgiving, and *koinonia*. When this motive prevails, there will be no need for pressure to give. The power of an inward expulsion in light of new inner life will produce a sense of stewardship that embraces all of life.

Chapter Five

The Kingdom of God

Without question, the central category of teaching in the ministry of Jesus Christ was the Kingdom of God. All understanding of His life and work must begin with a grasp of that Kingdom. A review of the synoptic Gospels demonstrates this clearly:

> Now after John was put in prison, Jesus came to Galilee, preaching the gospel of the Kingdom of God, and saying, "The time is fulfilled, and the Kingdom of God is at hand. Repent and believe in the gospel" (Mark 1:14-15).
>
> He went about all Galilee, teaching in their synagogues and preaching the gospel of the Kingdom (Matt. 4:23).

Interpretations of the Kingdom of God have varied over the centuries. From Augustine until the time of the reformers, the Kingdom was identified with the Church. Liberal Christian theology identified it with the Fatherhood of God, the "brotherhood" of man, and the value of the soul. Some, such as C. H. Dodd, have emphasized the Kingdom as an altogether present reality. Dispensationalists have posited that the Kingdom was delayed until the coming reign of Christ. Still others see the Kingdom as a reality inaugurated in the first Advent of Jesus and yet to be consummated in His Second Advent.

The Kingdom of God can best be understood by a careful understanding of the phrase *baseleia tou theou*. Behind this Greek phrase rests the Hebrew word *mālkûṭ*. The word carries the dynamic idea of the reign, rule, or sovereignty of God. For example: "The Lord has established His throne in heaven, and His kingdom rules over all" (Ps. 103:19). Hence, the Kingdom of God means the rule or reign of God.

Without question, this rule or reign of God found a new and exciting expression in the earthly ministry of Jesus. One of His most expressive statements concerning the presence of the Kingdom is that of Matt. 12:28: "But if I cast out demons by the Spirit of God, surely the Kingdom of God has come upon you." Surely one of Jesus' most characteristic acts was the exorcism of demons. He used this as a demonstration that the powers of the Kingdom had invaded human history.

Thus, all Jesus does is an expression of the present power of the reign of God. The parables are parables of the Kingdom, the miracles are the miracles of the Kingdom, and the stewardship of the present is the stewardship of the Kingdom. Jesus clearly stated to the Pharisees that the Kingdom was already in their midst, albeit in an unexpected form.

THE PARABLES OF STEWARDSHIP

Jesus' teaching concerning the Kingdom of God adopted the parabolic form as its main vehicle of expression. Although everything Jesus taught was in some sense an aspect of the Kingdom, the parables were the idiom of choice in His speaking of God's reign. Further, the parables seem to be the central mode of His teaching about stewardship.

The twentieth century witnessed a revolution in the under-standing of Jesus' parables. For centuries, the church interpret-ed the parables as allegories. Each detail of a parable was symbolic of some larger spiritual truth. This made a travesty of Jesus' intention in the parables. There followed the theory of Jülicher that parables contained "one main point." This approach tended to make the parables bland moralisms. This century witnessed a return to the parables as Jesus intended them. The parables are "effective" language that call for deci-sion on the part of the hearer. The parables draw the congrega-tion in and they are making a judgment on the characters in the parables before they realize it. The parables are best understood in existential terms. They speak of life in the world and the Kingdom in terms that relate with immediacy and timelessness to life. In that sense, the parables reverse the usual relationship between the text and the interpreter. Ordinarily, we think of the interpreter explaining the text. In the parables, the text explains the interpreter. It is not so much that the parables are dark and we bring light to them. It is more so that we are dark and the parables enlighten our lives.

The parables are particularly effective vehicles for teaching stewardship in that they are secular in their language. The para-bles are indeed earthly stories with a heavenly meaning. The characters and plots in the parables are almost all secular. There is an absence of the particularly theological or ecclesiastical. The parables are a parade of sowers, pearl merchants, plowmen, kings, crooks, con artists, laborers, and wedding guests. These very secular stories carry Jesus' interpretation of stewardship in life. The very nature of parabolic language underscores its appropriateness as a vehicle for stewardship stories.

We shall examine the parables of Jesus for the light they shed on His understanding of life as stewardship. Although virtually every parable touches directly or indirectly on stewardship in the Kingdom, we shall examine those that relate directly to that theme.

The Twin Parables of the Hidden Treasure and the Pearl (Matt. 13:44-46)

There is joy in the risk of the steward. The parable of the hidden treasure compares the reign of God to a plowman suddenly finding hidden treasure. The picture is that of a day laborer in Palestine plowing the field of an absentee landlord. Such fields sometimes contained a ceramic vessel holding buried treasure. In the landbridge of Palestine, invaders had repeatedly swept down from the surrounding empires. The biblical world knew no banks, safes, or deposit boxes. In many cases, temples performed banklike functions, taking deposits, holding valuables, and even making loans. But people didn't put their valuables in a temple during an invasion because it was sure to be raided. When the Hebrews saw an invader coming, they would hide treasure in tree trunks, walls, cisterns, or bury it in ceramic jars in open fields. Often the laborers were captured, never returned, or later forgot where they had hid the treasure.

A reality of life in Jesus' time was the sudden discovery of buried treasure. This has continued in the Middle East to this day. In Jesus' story a day laborer suddenly plows up a treasure jar. After opening it, he sees the glint of treasure inside the jar. Looking around furtively, he buries the jar again. Leaving the plow in the field, he sells everything he has and buys the field. This was all done with a sense of inward joy. His life was changed forever. Once a simple day laborer working for a *denarius*, he will now be a man of means and affluence. In Jesus' world, the law of the rabbis permitted the man to do just what he did without telling the owner of his find.

The Kingdom of God calls for risk just such as this man took. To know the rule of God is a treasure. Finding that treasure calls on the finder to liquidate everything in life that matters less and surrender it to have the treasure. As a teaching on stewardship, the message is twofold. First, the Christian must be willing to risk personal worth for the sake of the treasured message of the Kingdom. Yet this risk is taken in joy. It is joy like one who trades a plow for a treasure!

The parable of the pearl moves in a different atmosphere. Its hero is a pearl merchant on a grand scale. What he buys in the East he sells in Jerusalem. He visits the great pearl fisheries of the Persian Gulf looking for the most beautiful pearls. He is no mere shopkeeper—he is a pearl wholesaler seeking the finest pearls to retail elsewhere. He has pyramided his holdings into a pearl empire. On a given day, he suddenly discovers a pearl beyond all pearls he has ever seen. In response to the discovery, he liquidates his entire pearl holdings in order to buy this one pearl of perfect proportion.

At the point of stewardship, the Kingdom offers just such an opportunity. It is a once-in-a-lifetime opportunity. The call of Jesus always creates a crisis of value in the realm of stewardship. The pearl merchant gave up everything he valued for something that he suddenly valued more. There is no comparison between the Kingdom of God and the most valuable of human possessions. The emphasis rests on the suddenness and completeness of the person's decision. Without hesitation a person trades everything for the Kingdom. In the life of a Christian steward there comes a crisis in which the steward must recognize the call of Jesus to trade everything for the sake of the gospel. There must at least be that urgent sense of willingness to give whatever it takes for the Kingdom. The coming of the reign of God in a life changes the values of a lifetime. Out of joy and with urgency the steward gives up something once loved for something suddenly prized even more.

The Parable of the Talents (Matt. 25:14-30)

This parable and the similar parable of the pounds (Luke 19:11-28) call for a risk-taking investment of life in the Kingdom of God. Jesus compares the reign of God to this entire story of three stewards who were left a legacy by a lord leaving on a long journey to a far country. This absentee lord leaves a small fortune to the three stewards. To one he gives five golden talents, to another two, and to the one with the least capacity for risk he leaves one. The Greek word *talenta* has led to no small confusion in the interpretation of this parable. It has been translated into the English word "talent." We consider the word talent the description of some human capacity or gift for achievement or performance. This has led to a rather banal interpretation that "we should all use our talents for the Lord." No one would disagree with that as an application of the parable. But the interpretation of the parable has a far more radical reach.

The five-talent steward and the two-talent steward are actually window dressing to set off in relief the true antihero of the story—the one-talent steward. Even though he has less to lose than the others, he refuses to risk the investment of stewardship. While the others invested their legacy in the risk of the marketplace, the riskless steward buried his talent. He took an option that was not an option. He refused to risk that stuff of life given him by his lord.

Somewhere there is the story of an inland lad who all his life dreamed of going to sea on a tall-masted sailing ship. He slipped away from home and enlisted as an apprentice sailor. On the third day at sea, the captain commanded that he take the watch in the crow's nest. Halfway up the mast he froze. He had never been that high up in his life. He would not go up or down. He feared the height of the crow's nest above him. Yet at the same time he feared the ridicule of the sailors on the deck beneath him. He froze, moving neither up nor down.

This is the image of this frozen steward. He would neither disown his lord and throw away the talent nor risk it in the marketplace of life. In this regard he epitomizes many professing followers of Jesus. They would never disagree that His call deserves the stewardship of their time, talent, and treasure. But at the same time they are unwilling to take the risk that actualizes the stewardship.

Verse 19 is the turning point of the parable: "After a long time the lord of those servants came and settled accounts with them." Stewardship will always face a moment of personal accountability. The law of the Kingdom calls for an encounter with the Lord of the stewards. In the face of teaching that Jesus expected a short duration for His Kingdom before the end, it is of interest that this judgment took place "after a long time." This is more than apologizing for a delayed *parousia*. It presents a considerable expanse of history as the stage for stewardship, but an ultimate and certain encounter with the Lord of the stewards.

The five- and two-talent stewards doubled the legacy of their lord. They are commended for their faithfulness. They are given even more over which to be faithful. They are given an entrance into the joy of their lord. Their lord promises that they will be "ruler over many things." Faithfulness at one level of stewardship opens the door for more and greater faithfulness. This is a basic teaching of Jesus on stewardship. Faithfulness over what one has will be rewarded with the opportunity for more faithfulness in an even larger sphere. This is far from a mere reward theory of stewardship. To one who loves the Lord, the greatest joy is an increased opportunity to be steward over more. This presents the possibility of an infinitely expanding opportunity for stewardship in the life to come.

The Lord gave exactly the same commendation to the five-talent and two-talent servants. People vary in their endowment and capacity for risk. All those who cross the threshold of risk belong to the same order of heroes. There are no discounted servants.

The one-talent servant is nailed to his riskless living. Immediately, he blames his lord's own hardness and exacting expectations. Nothing warps our perspective on God like riskless living. His lord was anything but a tyrant. He was an expectant lord who loved to reward faithful stewards generously. The servant next blames his own fear of life (v. 25). In the Kingdom of God, fear is never an adequate excuse for failure in stewardship. The lord calls him *ponēros,* wicked (v. 26). This man is no adulterer or murderer. He is simply a cipher who failed to risk for his lord's kingdom. The word *ponēros* is used elsewhere for the very devil himself. There is something essentially evil about the sloth that refuses to risk for the master's kingdom. Further, the servant is lazy. The word suggests a sloth that is incarcerated in its own inertia and imprisoned in its own inability to move. Barth considered sloth the essence of sin. The man was frozen in his tracks and could not move toward stewardship. The most chilling judgment, however, is the blasting judgment, "Therefore take the talent from him, and give it to him who has ten talents" (v. 28). Here is a Kingdom principle of stewardship. Opportunities not seized for the Kingdom pass on to those who are willing to take the risk. The banality of risklessness yields a loss of even what one has. Those who risk for the Kingdom receive more to risk. Those who fail to risk lose even the little they hoard.

The unprofitable servant loses all opportunity, cast into outer darkness (v. 30). The parable is a tragedy of lost opportunity. Whereas some of Jesus' parables are comedies in the Greek sense—the protagonist moves from impossibility to possibility—this parable is a tragedy in the Greek sense. The central figure moved from a moment of possibility to a future of impossibility, all because of the failure to risk as a steward.

The Parable of the Sheep and Goats (Matt. 25:31-46)

According to Matthew, Jesus spoke these words on the same occasion as the parable of the talents. Whereas the talents relate to risk in order to serve the Kingdom, this parable speaks in terms of merciful deeds, the impact of which reach all the way to the Final Judgment. As stewards, we meet Christ incognito when we provide for the needs of hurting humans.

Jesus introduces Himself as the "Son of Man." This is His favorite self-designation. The phrase means more than the simple humanity of Jesus. In its fullest biblical sense against the backdrop of the Old Testament, it means one who comes to a state of exaltation by way of humiliation. As the One for others, Jesus reveals that final judgment will be rendered on the basis of evidence provided by actual deeds of mercy. Although we are saved by grace alone, in the New Testament the evidence of salvation at the Last Judgment is without exception based on actual deeds. This is the only place in the synoptic Gospels in which Jesus refers to Himself as King (v. 34). Here is a regal setting of the King surrounded by angels in the brilliance of glory.

At this judgment, the nations are gathered before His throne. Here every division of humanity disappears. We think of nations in terms of location, racial constituency, East or West, democratic or dictatorial, etc. In the Final Judgment, there are only "sheep on His right hand, but goats on the left" (v. 33). In the Holy Land sheep might be left uncovered at night, but goats might be taken in because they cannot stand the chill. In the day the flocks grazed together, but at night the shepherd separated sheep from goats. Against the backdrop of that pastoral custom, Jesus sets the Final Judgment of the world's nations. All nations will thus be divided into two camps.

The basis of this judgment is simple. The sheep showed by the stewardship of life acts of compassion and mercy through the use of life's resources. Six acts of compassion are named: feeding the hungry, slacking thirst, welcoming strangers with hospitality, clothing the ill-clad, and visiting the sick and the prisoners. These words were echoed by James, the half brother of Jesus: "Pure and undefiled religion before God and the Father is this: to visit orphans and widows in their trouble, and to keep oneself unspotted from the world" (James 1:27). Compassion for others expressed in a concrete stewardship of life demonstrates the reality of faith.

Noteworthy is the utter lack of self-consciousness on the part of the faithful stewards: "When did we see You a stranger and take You in, or naked and clothe You?" (Matt. 25:38). They did not recognize in the simple meeting of the needs of others less fortunate that they were serving Christ. Ivan Turgenev told of visiting a simple country church. One sat next to him that he felt must be Christ, so strong was the spiritual presence. Yet when he turned to look at the stranger, the face was so absolutely ordinary. He finally came to understand that it is in the ordinary needs of humankind that we see the face of Jesus Christ.[1] This lack of self-consciousness in giving represents a vital aspect of stewardship for Jesus. In the Sermon on the Mount He taught this: "When you do a charitable deed, do not let your left hand know what your right hand is doing" (Matt. 6:3). Giving should be with such an utter lack of self-congratulation, with such an unadorned unawareness that an act of generosity is taking place, that it should be as if one hand forgot the other.

The objects of this mercy are "one of the least of these My brethren." Some have stressed this to the literal identification of Jesus' brethren as the Jews. This misses the point of Matt. 12:50. Jesus' brethren are those who do the will of God. Wherever we care for those who are weak, disenfranchised, disinherited, abused, homeless, and powerless we meet the face of Jesus Christ.

The "goats" are those who omitted to care for others. They are not guilty of deeds of heinous conduct. They were simply those who did not see the face of Christ in the face of need. These are they that go away into "everlasting punishment" (v. 46). Those who did not recognize Christ incognito in the face of human need go to hell. This is the most somber and stern of stewardship parables. Today so many believers fear they will be abused or taken advantage of if they give to those in need around them. It would be ten thousand times better to be thus abused than to stand among those thus dismissed by Christ. No clearer teaching exists in the Word of God than that we will meet in eternity what we do with the resources of time.

The Parable of the Good Samaritan (Luke 10:25-37)

The word "compassion" in the Gospels is always used in connection with, about, or by Jesus Christ. This parable calls for compassion upon whoever needs it, without bounds. Stewardship expresses itself in the face of human need, and asks questions later. This parable has passed into the world's literature and has become such a byword that its interpretation has lost its bite. To understand its existential shock one must substitute for the wounded traveler a member of the Black Muslims and for the Good Samaritan a member of the Ku Klux Klan. The parable gives a shocking answer to the question, "Who is my neighbor?"

The obvious irony of the parable is the two Hebrew religionists that passed by the victim. Indeed, the rabbis had taught that one should push a heretic or renegade into the ditch, not pull him out! It has sometimes been taught that the priest and the Levite passed by the man because they thought him a corpse, and would have been ritually unclean had they touched him. The Samaritan was a man with half a Bible and mixed blood. He was the incarnation of the obnoxious to the Jew. Among other lessons from this immortal tale, it teaches that the unlikely one among us might be the real steward. Jesus moved the questioning theologian from the hypothetical to the actual, from the theological to the ethical (v. 36). Jesus will not allow us the luxury of theoretical questions in the matter of stewardship. You become the steward in the ditch when pouring oil into the wounds of a wounded brother. You become the steward when you put the hurt one on your own transportation, spend the night with him, and even pay someone else to care for him until you return. You will pay the bill. Stewardship is extravagant love. What if the man in the ditch is a con man? What if the innkeeper inflates your bill? These obvious matters of practical concern do not concern the steward in this parable. He is a person for the hurt one.

One college professor put on a shocking demonstration of this parable. On the day he planned to teach this story to his class, he staged a similar accident on the college courtyard outside the building. A student writhed on the manicured lawn of the college as if he had just been hurt. He did this immediately before the bell sounding the beginning of class. The rushing students ran around him, and in one case actually stepped over him to get to class and study this parable. You can imagine the shock to the class when the professor revealed his tactic.

Stewardship always falls victim to theoretical discussions. Should one give to this program or that, this building fund or that other cause, this institution or that ministry? Here Jesus concretizes the question by confronting the steward with the need immediately, existentially before him. The theoretical vanishes. The immediate and the practical slaps the steward in the face with its reality. Some people can never join a church fellowship because they can never find the right mix of people and doctrine. For the same reason, some can elude stewardship for a lifetime because they can never find the right circumstances to give. Jesus here pushes us into the crisis of the moment. Be a steward to the need obviously and immediately before you.

The Parable of the Unjust Steward (Luke 16:1-13)

That this parable provokes more debate about Jesus' intention than His other parables has become a byword of biblical scholarship. In it, Jesus seems to comment on the deception of a suddenly dismissed employee against his former employer. The shock value of the story should not be overlooked. Jesus often told stories that shocked His listeners into the acceptance of a certain truth.

Archibald Hunter helps us understand this parable by putting it into another culture, the Scots culture, with which Hunter was familiar:

> There was a dishonest laird, said Jesus, who had a dishonest factor (in Scotland a factor is someone who runs the estate of a laird, absentee landlord). When someone whispered to the laird that his factor was slowly ruining him—possibly by feathering his own nest out of the estate—the laird summoned him and faced him with his villainy. "You had better turn in your accounts," he said, "for I mean to sack you."
>
> The factor wasted no time in cursing the laird or those who had "split" on him. He did a bit of quick thinking. "I'm going to get my books," he reflected, "but what am I to do afterwards? Manual labor is not for me—I'm too soft. And I'm too proud to take to the road and beg. But, wait, I think I have it. Even if I am going to lose my job, I can still see a way of keeping in with my friends."
>
> So he summoned the chief farmers who had loans from the estate. When the first appeared, the factor asked, "What is our debt to the laird?" "A thousand gallons of oil." "Very well," said the factor, "call it five hundred." To the next farmer he said, "How much do you owe?" "A thousand bushels of wheat." "Right" said the factor, "take your pen and change the figure from a ten to an eight." And so, by deliberately falsifying the accounts, the factor put the two farmers under a lasting obligation to himself and secured their future friendship and a roof over his head.[2]

When placing the story into another context from that of the New Testament, we see just how shocking the story really is. A criminal, threatened with exposure, acts shrewdly to secure his own future security. Most commentators consider the primary intent of Jesus in this parable to commend the urgent shrewdness with which the steward acted. Faced with a calamity, he acted with a quick, energetic, creative, and decisive strategy. In matters of stewardship, Jesus expects His followers to act with just such decisiveness. Jesus does not commend the duplicity of the steward; He does commend the decisiveness of the steward. The coming of Jesus Christ into the world and into anyone's life creates a crisis. In the face of that crisis, we should all act with an urgent shrewdness in matters of stewardship. We do not have forever.

The Lord Jesus goes on to add a number of other applications from this story. Some scholars take the viewpoint that Matthew or the early church added these comments by way of homiletic exhortation. Others prefer to see these words as those of the Lord Jesus amplifying the lessons of the parable. What are these applications?

Christians Should Act Intensely as God's Stewards. Christians should act as wisely in the stewardship of their means for God's Kingdom as do the secularists in building their own kingdom. "For the sons of this world are more shrewd in their generation than the sons of light" (Luke 16:8b). Those who belong to this *kosmos*, the world organized against God and God's people, act with a greater sagacity in their secular pursuit of wealth than Christians do in their stewardship of resources for the Kingdom. Consider the entrepreneur or investor who constantly and energetically seeks opportunities, reads company profiles, pours over profit and loss statements, and seeks any opening to exploit the profitability of a new business. The comparative lack of energy, creativity, and shrewdness employed by Christians in providing for the Kingdom of God is a scalding contrast. Whereas the "sons of this world" make money for secular purposes in a temporal world, the "sons of light" are responsible for stewardship relating to eternal matters. Yet the worldlings act with a decisiveness and intensity that shame those of the Kingdom. Why is this? The world is simply too much with us. It is the rare exception of a person who can relate to the invisible realities of God's Kingdom with the same intensity as those who deal with the visible realities of business.

Christians Should Invest in the World. Christians should use money in this world in a way that provides an abundant welcome in the age to come. "Make friends for yourselves by unrighteous mammon, that when you fail, they may receive you into an everlasting home" (Luke 16: 9). What believers do with material wealth in this age does affect the welcome—not the fact, but the quality—of the believer's life in the age to come. This simple reality should not provoke a debate about "law" and "grace" or "faith" and "works." Of course we are saved by grace through faith. Yet it is also a stark reality that our capacity for enjoyment of life in the world to come relates to our present investment in that world. That this belonged to the core of Jesus' teachings rests beyond all debate. The Kingdom person can store up treasure in heaven on the basis of what that person does with treasure on Earth (Matt. 6:19-20).

Consider a simple comparison. One person of modest means makes a pledge to the new civic performing arts center.

That pledge is a real sacrifice in terms of available wealth. On the other hand, a person of great means makes only a token contribution, and that under the obligation of social pressure. The night comes for the first performance in the new center. The orchestra begins its prelude. The symphony performs flawlessly. Who do you suppose has a deeper, fuller, and more fulfilling experience of that evening? The one who gave the pledge or the one who only gave a token? Of course, that to which we give is that which means the most to us.

Christians Should be Faithful. Christians must be faithful in small things before they can be faithful in greater things; those who fail in smaller stewardship will fail in larger ones (vv. 10-11). Again, this is an abiding principle of Jesus' teaching about stewardship. Life is a unity. If a person fails in faithfulness regarding small things, that person would fail in faithfulness in the matter of large things. All of life is preparation for a larger stage. "One's true identity and loyalties find their expression in what a person does with small things (and which he also likewise does with large things). His faithfulness or dishonesty appears throughout—in his ordinary life or in his spiritual life."[3] The casual worshiper who tips God a dollar in the offering plate would do proportionately no more than that if he had greater wealth.

Christians Must be Faithful in One Arena to Enter Another. "If you have not been faithful in what is another man's, who will give you what is your own?" (v. 12). This verse contemplates a future opportunity in stewardship where the Lord Jesus would give each steward more individual responsibility and ownership in Kingdom work. If an individual cannot be faithful now in managing the affairs of an absentee but returning

Lord, how much less would that person be faithful over an even more personally invested responsibility later. When a Christian, for example, is given a committee position in the church or a class to teach, there is a stewardship involved on the human level. The pastor or minister has given to that person a portion of responsibility for the health of the church. If such a person cannot be responsible for a trust shared in time, how much less could such a person be responsible for a trust given in eternity?

The Christian Cannot be Equally Loyal to God and Material Wealth. The Christian cannot give ultimate loyalty both to God and to material wealth (v. 13). Life can only have one ultimate loyalty. There is more difference between one and two than there is between two and ten thousand in terms of qualitative difference. There is a uniqueness about singular commitment that cannot be diluted. No person can poise in equal balance between commitment to God and to money. Jesus indicates with a true psychology that such an equipoise between two masters will only lead to one being despised and the other being loved. A resentful abhorrence grows toward the competing master when a heart is divided. God or money. Make a choice between masters, says Jesus.

The Parable of the Six Brothers (Luke 16:19-31)

Usually called the parable of the rich man and Lazarus, this parable is really about the fate of six brothers. We sometimes promote to the title role someone in the parables who is in reality a supporting actor. Lazarus is the only named character in any of Jesus' parables. His name means "God helps" in Aramaic. Similar stories to this were familiar to Jesus' generation. The characters in this story reflected well-known folklore. Jesus simply gave it a surprise ending.

In all likelihood this story was told to the Sadducees, the liberal rationalists of Jesus' world. They were materialistic. They believed that all that exists is this world. Humans die like dogs. This led them in some instances to a cynical hedonism. They had a choke hold on the religious institutions in Jerusalem. Concern for the poor was not on their agenda. Jesus held this parable up to them as a mirror.

One of six brothers revels in an affluent life. He wears expensive purple clothing, linen underwear from Egypt, and enjoys the life of a gourmet connoisseur. It can be inferred that he was an immoral man, but this is not explicitly stated. He is a man who lives in detachment from the poverty of those just under his nose. While he feasts at his table, another man starves outside the secured gate of his mansion. Lazarus is a street person. Not only is he crippled, but also his body erupts in ulcerous sores from a skin disease. No one likes to look at a Lazarus, not the least the man in his mansion. As for Lazarus, he wanted to eat the bread crumbs on which the dinner guests of the rich man wiped their hands.

Thus, the visible world presents itself. This tableau could represent thousands of such scenes around the world in every century. Suddenly, however, the invisible world intrudes. It is a shocking reversal of fortune. One can imagine two funerals. The rich man is eulogized, buried in his purple robe and linen underpants. In all likelihood he was remembered for what he had done in the community. The beggar died in the streets, the wild dog packs licking the sores that devastated his emaciated body. The Jewish theology of Jesus' day would have consigned him to hell. He must have done some terrible thing to live and die licked by dogs. Wealth meant the blessing of God, and poverty the sign of divine wrath.

Evidently, death does something for myopia. The rich man suddenly sees someone he had never noticed, Lazarus. Now Lazarus is seated at the place of honor in the heavenly feast— right next to Father Abraham. This ulcerous beggar that held no interest for the rich man in the visible world becomes the focus of his intense interest in the next. One is tempted to say that none of the rich man's friends were to be seen in the heavenly world; his network had disappeared. The only contact he had in heaven was one he never cared to cultivate on Earth, Lazarus. The rich man is in Hades. This is a picture of the intermediate state before the Final Judgment. The New Testament makes a clear distinction between Hades and *gehenna*, the permanent location of the lost dead. Since the rich man knows that he is in an intermediate state, he appeals to Father Abraham. He now wants Lazarus to dip his finger in water and cool his withered, parched tongue. The man who would not lift a finger to help Lazarus suddenly wants Lazarus to lift a finger to help him.

Abraham takes Lazarus off the hook. Providence will not permit Lazarus to be demeaned into a water boy for the man who would not have given Lazarus the time of day. An impassable chasm yawns between the two. Interestingly, on this small stage everybody can see everybody else. To what extent Jesus is giving a tour of life beyond one cannot say. Two things are certain: there is a life beyond, and what we did with wealth in this life will figure greatly in our final disposition. Those who lived in affluence and disregard for the needy around them will find themselves in a total reversal of circumstances. Although they enjoyed a few good meals in the visible life, they will spend eternity wanting a glass of water in the invisible world. Jesus never permits us to get theoretical about stewardship. We can debate welfare, poverty, laziness, and our responsibility endlessly. The only appropriate response to this parable is to find someone in need immediately and express our faith through the relief of another person's need. If we turn this into a debate about faith and works, we will demonstrate that we have neither. Jesus always leaves us with actual cases.

The actual intent of the parable appears at its surprise ending. Suddenly, this rich man becomes an evangelist for his five brothers, still on Earth. We sometimes hear the boast, "I don't mind going to hell; all my friends will be there." That is not the sentiment of the rich man. His misery did not love company. He first wishes that Lazarus would appear to his brothers in a dream or vision. He is certain that his brothers would repent from their inhumane lifestyle, a reflection of his own. Abraham gives him a jolt. Even if someone were to be physically raised from the dead, the appearance would not lead to repentance on the part of those who will not heed the word of God. If they will not hear "Moses and the prophets," they will not heed a resurrected Lazarus. Of such hardness is the impenitent heart. One of the most famous preachers of this century expressed the same. According to him, he had witnessed the "deathbed" conversion of several wealthy individuals who repented on the edge of eternity. When suddenly their condition improved, they forgot their "repentance" and returned to the life they had lived, some of them living for years with no recollection of their "conversion."

This most dramatic of parables should stimulate us with the urgency to be stewards in the face of human need. In all of the parables there is an element of urgency that the crisis comes with the Kingdom of God. This parable should move us with urgency to find Lazarus today.

SUMMARY OF THE PARABOLIC TEACHING ON STEWARDSHIP

In some respect, virtually all of Jesus' parabolic teachings touch on some aspect of stewardship. The six above demonstrate the major themes.

- The parable of the treasure and the pearl teaches the urgency of action in the face of the Kingdom's demand for stewardship.
- The parable of the talents calls for a risk in stewardship in the face of the reign of God.
- The parable of the sheep and goats demonstrates the judgment of God on our misuse of resources in the face of human need.
- The parable of the good Samaritan reveals the concrete necessity of meeting the immediate need at hand as the expression of stewardship.
- The parable of the unjust steward demonstrates the shrewd use of material in this world to prepare for the world to come.
- The parable of the six brothers echoes the urgent crisis to relieve human need at our very doorstep through stewardship.

By the very nature of their language, the parables pull us into the situation, and in passing judgment on the characters therein we judge ourselves.

THE TEACHINGS OF JESUS IN RELATIONSHIP TO THE MATERIAL WORLD

Even a cursory reading of the Gospels reveals in Jesus a freedom from the tyranny of the material. Although He never had much, what He had satisfied Him. In the fifty to sixty individual days recorded in the Gospels, Jesus revealed no anxiety, obsession, or distraction by the material aspects of life. The Sermon on the Mount, as a summary of Jesus' teaching about the Kingdom, warns repeatedly against the tyranny of things and the supremacy of His Kingdom. "Seek first the kingdom of God and His righteousness, and all these things shall be added to you" (Matt. 6:33). The things of which Jesus speaks refer to the material support of life, food, and clothes. We are to put the reign of God in our life first, and the material necessities of life will care for themselves.

Jesus' statement about worry as it relates to the material necessities of life is a keystone in His statement of stewardship (Matt. 6:25-34). Jesus begins with a command that His disciples stop the habit of being distracted or divided by care about the material aspects of life. The Greek verb *merizō* refers to anything that divides or distracts. The object of their distraction was their life and their body. More particularly, they were distracted with worry about the food and drink that sustain life and the clothing that they put on the body to sustain its life. Jesus counters this with a masterful lordly logic: Life is more than food and the body is more than clothing. If God gave the greater gift, life, God will certainly give the lesser gift, the food to sustain that life. If God gave the greater gift, the body, God will certainly give the lesser gift, the clothing to protect it. It is a principle that God's greater gifts include the lesser. When

God led the people out of Egypt in the Exodus, the greater gift of liberation included the lesser gifts of the *manna* and the water to sustain God's people in the wilderness. It is the assumption of faith that God will care for the temporal needs of God's people until God's work for them on Earth is finished.

Jesus then argues from the lesser to the greater. If God feeds birds that are of minimal value, how much more will God feed God's own children? If God adorns perishing wildflowers with beauty when their destination is the communal oven, how much more will God clothe God's own children? There is absolutely no need for God's children to worry over the material aspects of life: "Your heavenly Father knows that you need all these things" (v. 32). Jesus pictures the relatively short Jew comparing his height with the Roman that towers over him. Worry however much he might, he cannot add any to his physical height (v. 27). If we cannot affect anything so personal and permanent as our stature by worry, we certainly cannot change the material circumstances of life by such worry. Such worry characterizes the life of the pagan Gentiles (v. 32). There should be a distinct difference between the people of the Kingdom and the gentile world. That difference is found in the command "Seek first the kingdom of God." When the reign of God is the priority of life, it evacuates concerns about the material aspect of life.

Although this seems to be advice about the prohibition of worry, it is in reality the basis of life as a steward. No one who is consumed with distracting, cankering care about his own life can give time, talent, and treasure to the Kingdom. Why do professing believers withhold a life of stewardship from the Kingdom? Is it not because they are distracted with distrust toward God's ability or willingness to sustain them in the material aspect of life? If we are certain that God will care for us even as we care for God, we are liberated to practice a life of stewardship for God's Kingdom.

Giving as a Reflection of Relationships (Matt. 5:23-24)

The Sermon on the Mount contains the Six Great Contrasts between the oral interpretation of the Law and Jesus' application of the Law in His Kingdom. As part of His teaching against hatred, Jesus points to the offering time at the Temple. For the Jew, one of life's most sacred moments was when the animal sacrifice or its monetary equivalent was brought to the Temple. Jesus pictures one such worshiper in the very act of lifting up the sacrifice to hand it to the priest. At that moment the worshiper remembers that fellowship has been breached with another. He is to do what the rabbis would consider a sacrilege, drop his gift on the Temple floor. Immediately he is to find the offended brother and make things right. Then and only then is he to return to the Temple and give the offering.

Here Jesus commends that giving which is done in an atmosphere of fellowship. The very Greek word *koinonia* can be interpreted as "Christian fellowship" or the concrete gift that is the expression of that fellowship. Giving to God never replaces the need for fellowship with one another. God does not desire giving to the exclusion of being right with the other believer.

Unself-Conscious Giving (Matt. 6:1-4)

As in all things, Jesus goes to the heart of the motive in giving. Giving should not be for public recognition, but for the private observation of God. Jesus accuses the ostentatious givers of His day of giving in such a way as to call attention to the giver and the gift (6:2). "Sound the trumpet" might refer to the way that a gift was given in the peculiar receptacle at the place of worship. A gift could be so given that it would "zing" around the trumpet-shaped receptacle and call attention to itself. The result of such giving is that it has its own reward. The giver wanted attention; he got it. That is all. The giver got what he wanted, the praise of other humans. He will have no reward from God.

Giving should be with such an utter unself-consciousness that it should be as if the left hand does not know what the right hand is doing (v. 3). An utter lack of awareness is implied. The act of giving should be so centered upon God and the need of the other that the very possibility of self-congratulation—no less the applause of others—is not even a matter of conscious thought. Kingdom people are to practice giving in secret, literally *kruptos*, as if in a crypt. God sees, and God will reward openly (v. 4).

Principles of Jesus' Teaching About The Material

Jesus desired that His followers be free from the tyranny of things and so be free to be concerned about the needs of others. Jesus continually warns against the tyranny of things in the believer's life. Rather than things dominating the individual's life, Jesus taught that the sovereign reign of God should be the first concern of life (Matt. 6:33). The attitude of a person toward possessions is a test of the vitality of faith. Jesus insisted that the reign of God brooks no rival in the heart of humans. God requires a singleness of heart. "No one can serve two masters: for either he will hate the one and love the other, or else he will be loyal to the one and despise the other. You cannot serve God and mammon" (Matt. 6:24). The word translated as "serve" must hold the full significance "be a slave of." Life simply cannot be mastered both by God and the obsessive pursuit of riches. Jesus does not say that a person cannot be rich and also serve God. The significant thing is how much riches matter to the person. If the pursuit of riches has been the central exploit of life, it rules out the Kingdom.

Jesus does not teach that it is a sin to make or have money. He does emphatically warn against placing trust in money. He warns against the seductive quality of wealth. There is an interesting dialectic in the life of Jesus. On the one hand, Jesus had friends with money and accepted their hospitality. It is clear that the Lazarus family of Bethany were people of some means. On the other hand, Jesus told one young man to sell all that he had and give it to the poor (Mark 10:21). The most significant thing in the young man's life was his wealth. Jesus gave a specific medication for a specific disease. Jesus did not tell everyone everywhere to sell all that they have. He did tell one rich person to do so. Jesus spoke frankly of the impossibility of the rich person entering heaven. The famous "eye of the needle" statement speaks of a literal needle, not a gate in the walls of Jerusalem (Mark 10:25). Jesus often resorted to hyperbole when speaking an unpopular truth. His teaching stood in stark contrast to the Jews who considered possessions a distinctive evidence of divine favor. Jesus did state that the rich man could be saved by the power of God (Mark 10:27). The attitude one has toward wealth can become either an occasion of stewardship or a damnation in life.

Jesus and Covetousness

Jesus warned against covetousness as if it were a malignancy of the soul. When a young man demanded a share of inheritance from his brother, Jesus warned sternly against covetousness. The Greek word *phulassesthe* reflects a life that guards against covetousness (Luke 12:15). The emphasis rests on the rigorous protection of life from covetousness. The words seem not aimed at just the young man but at all humanity. Covetousness can be present in very small matters and petty concerns. One does not have to be the rich fool to be guilty of covetousness. Covetousness can be the desire to have things merely for the sake of having them or it can be the desire to have the thing that belongs to another. At its worse form, covetousness does not want the other thing but does not want another to have it either. We must understand that things are temporal and belong to God. Nothing lasts but God. All monuments of humans are crumbling monuments. All empires will one day be falling empires.

Jesus further warns against a distraction over the gaining of material needs. How many people live life in a perpetual panic over the means to gain the material needs of life. In Matt. 6:25, Jesus used the Greek imperative *me meremnate*, which forbids the dividing or distracting care that comes from worry. He points to the lilies of the field and rock pigeons in the air around Galilee as evidence that God cares. No bird ever got an ulcer over the stock market. The only alternative to worry over things is trust in God.

Ownership of Property

Jesus did not oppose the ownership of private property. He stayed at Peter's home in Capernaum and with Mary, Martha, and Lazarus near Bethany. When Zaccheus proposed to give away half of his fortune, Jesus did not renounce him for not giving it all up (Luke 19:1-10). Rather, Jesus announced, "Today is salvation come to this house" (Luke 19:9). The fact that Jesus and the Twelve had a common purse does not indicate communism or opposition to private possessions. It was likely a matter of convenience, as one leader in a group of businessmen will carry the company money.

Jesus did not oppose the normal processes of making a living. An all but universal tradition indicates that Jesus supported His mother, brothers, and sisters by work as a carpenter. Later the needs of Jesus and the Twelve were supported by friends of Jesus who earned their money by work. The acquisition of wealth, however, must be done in a way that is commensurate with the values of the Kingdom.

Behind all of this teaching rests the truth that ultimate ownership belongs to God. For mortal humans it borders on the ridiculous to claim that anything one owns actually belongs to the one who owns it. We are tenants, not landlords. God said to the rich fool, "Fool! This night your soul will be required of you; then whose will those things be which you have provided?" (Luke 12:20). The Greek word *apaitousin* reflects the demand that something be returned. The rich fool not only did not own his barns, he did not own his own soul. He had to return the soul to God whence it came.

In contrast to this, Jesus emphasized that true treasure should be laid up in heaven. A person can so invest life on Earth that the person builds up treasure in heaven. Persons are not to "treasure up treasures on Earth" (Matt. 6:19-21). The deliberate pleonasm underscores the truth. Wealth was often kept in the form of precious garments. In the silence of the night, the stealthy moth could ruin the work of years. Rust could taint precious metals. There were certain vapors close to the Dead Sea that could even leave a tarnishing effect on gold. Thieves could easily dig through the adobe walls of the humble home, reach through with grasping hands, and take what they wished. The repetition of "treasure up treasures in heaven" makes the reality and the significance all the more cogent. The safest possible place for treasure is in heaven. By investing life in those going to heaven one enriches oneself in the heavenly treasure. Those who claim that this is a low motive are more spiritual than Jesus.

Jesus considers attitude toward possessions to be one of the most significant indicators of spiritual life. His followers are to flee covetousness. They are to so live on Earth that they store up treasures in the life beyond.

Giving for the Support of the Kingdom

Jesus never lessened the expectations of God's Law; He intensified those expectations. Jesus' teaching about tithing followed the same direction of all of His teaching: "Do not think that I came to destroy the Law or the Prophets. I did not come to destroy, but to fulfill" (Matt. 5:17). *Plerōsai* can mean to enforce or to express in its full significance. What murder was in the old covenant hatred is in the new (Matt. 5:21-22a). Jesus moved from the outward act to the inward attitude. His direction always moved from the external to the internal. He disdained the outward ritual in favor of the inward spiritual. That someone might give 10 percent and do as one might with the other 90 percent is an idea abhorrent to Jesus. Jesus' direction was always from the lesser to the greater, the lower to the higher, the lighter to the heavier. Love does not seek to give the minimum. With the motivation of love, the followers of Jesus will always be generous.

The widow who gave two mites represents Jesus' commen-dation of stewardship (Mark 12:41-44). She gave all that she had. She could have kept one mite for herself. She gave both. While the net amount of her gift was small, Jesus indicated that she had given more than all the rest. Jesus gives His strongest approval to this type of sacrificial giving. Jesus commended her while He was standing near the Temple treasury watching peo-ple give. Without doubt, many more affluent brought a tithe or more. There was such a way of giving in the Temple receptacle that it made a great noise. Jesus was not impressed with the ostentation of that giving.

In the same way, Mary of Bethany earned the commenda-tion of Jesus for her giving (Mark 14:3-9 and parallels). The ointment that Mary poured on Jesus was among the costliest oil available in the Roman world. It was available only to the wealthiest. It might have been an heirloom of Mary's family. Her act brought immediate criticism as extravagant. Yet Jesus looked beyond that criticism to commend Mary for her loving sacrifice. In breaking the alabaster bottle, she broke that which could not be resealed. It was another way of demonstrating the irreversible totality of her action.

Stewardship also included the practice of almsgiving for the poor. Jesus approved the practice, but warned against doing it in an ostentatious way. There is always the temptation of display in giving. Jesus does not insist on complete secrecy, but He does expect the absence of a show.

The Responsibility for Possessions Not Given

What does Jesus say of the remaining portion which is retained by the giver rather than specifically given to the work of the

Kingdom or alms? For many, to give a mere tithe leaves an enormous amount of money left in one's possession. Jesus did not say a great deal about the management of our money, but what He did say gives principles to follow in the stewardship of that which we keep as well as that which we give.

It might be easier to give everything away than to manage wisely that which one has: "To divest oneself at once of all property might be far easier than to expend it wisely and well, but the latter can be the use of a talent received from above and involving lifelong responsibility."[4] The parable of the shrewd steward suggests the intensity with which one should manage what one has for the sake of the Kingdom. The steward is an example of prudence and resourcefulness. Jesus commends the steward's foresight and intelligence. The steward used what was available to him in a prudent and clever manner. He used wealth to make friends in the day he would no longer be a steward. The steward is to use money in such a way as to make friends in and with the Kingdom of God. The faithful use of wealth on Earth will be rewarded with true spiritual riches being trusted to the steward.

Among those aspects which Jesus demands of the money we keep is care for the family. Jesus denounced the practice of declaring money *kōrban* and thus refusing to care for the needs of aging parents:

> He repudiated with unmitigated scorn the subterfuge by which, even in the name of religion, a son was allowed to escape his obligations to his indigent parents—for a son had merely to declare that the funds needed for their support were to be regarded as "dedicated," in order to absolve himself from all filial responsibility (Mark 7:9-13).[5]

Such laws as the Law of *kōrban* had no grounds in the original revelation of God's Law on Sinai. They were an oral accretion, and a self-serving one at that, to God's self-disclosure under the Old Covenant. That attitude of Jesus can clearly be seen in caring for His own mother while dying on the Cross. Giving to God does not preclude one from the most basic responsibilities, the support of aging or infirm parents.

Jesus had comparatively little to say of support for the state. Where He did speak, He spoke with a clarity and authority [Mark 12:14-27]. The Pharisees issued a challenge to Jesus concerning the payment of the tribute money. The tax in question was the poll tax or *tributum capitis* levied directly on those under Roman rule. The question was intended to be a trick. If Jesus identified with the Jewish nationalists He would offend the Romans and be considered treasonous. If Jesus identified with the Romans, He would scandalize the Jewish nationalists and be considered a traitor to His own people who had suffered at the hands of Rome. With divine wisdom Jesus responded that they must pay their ruler what is due to him. Citizenship has obligations. Jesus used the Greek word *apodote*, which does refer to the payment of a debt. It implies the repayment of what is due, giving back to God that which belongs to God. Jesus sets the two obligations side by side without conflict. One should not interfere with the other.

Central to Jesus' teaching on sharing was the use of possessions to care for the poor. Jesus gave great emphasis to the responsibility for such care. His teachings on the subject are so pointed that they have produced two opposite reactions. On the one hand, some have discounted His teachings as being too idealistic to work in the real world. On the other hand, some have made the "social gospel" the only gospel. Once again, this is not an either/or question. There can be no question that Jesus intended those who are more affluent to be generous to those who are burdened with need. Central to the message and ministry of Jesus was His concern for the poor. No amount of denial or manipulation of exegesis can paper over the obvious fact that Jesus expected His church to care for the poor. As noted above, the parable of the six brothers (Luke 16:19-31) does not comment on the evil of possessions or the nature of life in the world to come. It is, however, a parable showing the necessity of care for the poor on the part of Kingdom people. The rich man was not condemned for being rich. He was condemned for the neglect of Lazarus.

By application, every Christian should seek opportunities directly to relieve the needs of the poor in his or her arena of life. There is no substitute for this direct compassion toward the poor who are under our very noses. Today there are ways to make determination between the deserving poor and those who are deadbeats and parasites on society because they will not work. Most cities have charitable agencies with registries indicating the poor who really need help.

Another aspect of material stewardship is direct and immediate help to those who are in distress. The parable of the good Samaritan (Luke 10:25-37) dramatically points to that person in distress on our very road of life. We are to give unqualified help to that person in the midst of emergency. In that regard anyone must be considered a neighbor. There is no way to rationalize the open-ended nature of this expectation. Distress is where one finds it. That is the place to relieve it. If the Christian errs, the error should be in favor of helping rather than withholding.

Such help for the poor and distressed is further to be without expectation of the favor being returned (Luke 14:12-14).

Jesus identifies Himself with those in need. A concern for the needs of others is a concern for Christ (Matt. 25:31-46). We meet Christ in the other. When we see Christ we will be asked of our care for the other.

GIVING IN THE EARLY CHURCH

It rests beyond this survey of stewardship to give an exhaustive treatment of stewardship in the New Testament. Several passages are, however, representative of those themes in the life of the earliest Christian community. The first great statement of stewardship in the earliest church occurred in connection with the experience of Pentecost (Acts 2-4). On that occasion of the Jewish feast, Peter preached and thousands were converted. Many of those were from out of town, far from home, and suddenly part of the new Christian community in Jerusalem. Evidently, in light of the new faith, some among them stayed at Jerusalem for a significant amount of time. The Hellenic, Greek-speaking Jews of the Diaspora found themselves away from home in a Hebrew-speaking culture at Jerusalem. This situation created the need for a system of care in the earliest church.

In light of this there was a community of goods: "Now all who believed were together, and had all things in common, and sold their possessions and goods, and divided them among all, as anyone had need" (Acts 2:44-45). This has sometimes been interpreted as a system of communism in the early church in which private property was divested and all was held in common. It is unlikely that this was the case. The verb tenses indicate that it was from time to time, when need called for it, that the members would sell property and contribute to the relief of other members in need. This necessity was brought about because of the peculiar circumstances in Jerusalem at that time. The Hebrews who converted to Christianity were immediately cut off from the care of the Synagogue and were ostracized from society. They would have lost home, family, and in some cases vocation. These peculiar circumstances led to the unusual actions in Jerusalem by the Pentecostal Church. It is nowhere mandated in Acts or else-where that the church require a community of goods in which individual members are divested of all property and the sum is kept for the good of the whole.

Yet at the same time, we must recognize the principle implied. Members of the Body of Christ must radically care for one another in times of need. If the Church errs, it should err on the side of care for those in need rather than avoidance or overqualification of those that the Church helps. The experi-ence of the Jerusalem Church indicates a timeless principle of care for the needy in the church fellowship. No church can turns its back on needs in its very membership and be in conti-nuity with the New Testament model for the church.

THE OFFERING FOR THE RELIEF OF THE JERUSALEM SAINTS

One of the concrete and contextual studies on stewardship in the New Testament treats the offering for the believers in Jerusalem. Certain prophets traveled from Jerusalem to Antioch with a message of coming famine (Acts 11:27-30). The response from the Antioch Christian community is instructive. The disciples there decided to send relief to the Jerusalem believers. This was according to the ability of each disciple. They sent Barnabas and Saul with the relief. A great offering for the relief of the poor Christians in Jerusalem became a centerpiece of Paul's ministry. He not only wanted to relieve the needs in Jerusalem, he also wanted to cement Gentile and Jewish Christianity by means of the offering. It became a great obsession of Paul's ministry. He urged the Corinthian Christians to store up their gifts for the offering so there would be no more collection when he came. He in turn motivated the Roman Church by pointing to the generosity and intention of the Greeks: "For it pleased those from Macedonia and Achaia to make a certain contribution for the poor who are among the saints who are in Jerusalem" (Rom. 15:27). Here we see a grand scheme or vision for stewardship. Paul wished to relieve real human need. He also wished to do it in a way that would break down barriers in the early church. He used the need in Jerusalem to stimulate the Greeks to give, and then used the Greek example to stimulate the Romans.

It is thus a biblical principle to use the example of steward-ship on the part of some to motivate others. Paul indicates another principle of giving in the same context: "For if the Gentiles have been partakers of their spiritual things, their duty is also to minister to them in material things" (Rom. 15:27). It becomes a principle that those who minister spiritually have the right of support materially from those they have edified. This should not be the motive of Christian service. From the standpoint of those thus helped, it should be their desire to sup-port those who spiritually helped them.

In connection with this offering for the Jerusalem saints, Paul gave some of his most pointed teaching on stewardship. Giving is as grace. "We make known to you the grace of God bestowed on the churches of Macedonia" (2 Cor. 8:1). Giving is a ministry of the Holy Spirit wrought out in personal experience and outworked in practical expression. Far from a legalistic expectation based on unwilling extraction, giving is a work of grace in the heart of the believer. Paul used the generous giving of the Northern Macedonian Greeks to motivate the giving of the more reluctant southern Corinthian Greeks. "In a great trial of affliction the abundance of their joy and their deep poverty abounded in the riches of their liberality" (2 Cor. 8:2). The Macedonians gave out of circumstances of *thlipsis*. The Greek word indicates pressure that grinds. It could be used of the pressure that ground grain in a gristmill or that crushed grapes in a grape vat. Something about the circumstances of Greek Christians in Macedonia had created a situation of grinding pressure. It might have been economic, political, or religious persecution. Further, they were *ptōkoi*. That word for poverty indicates a people who faced a cringing poverty that bent them down. There are certainly levels of poverty. Those Greeks knew a "down to the bottom" kind of poverty. Yet in the midst of all of those difficulties, they gave generously to the offering of relief for Jerusalem.

It is an anomaly of American charitable and religious giving that the poorest in America give the largest percent of their income to such causes.

Further, Paul makes it explicitly clear that grace giving does not produce equal gifts, but it does produce equal sacrifice (2 Cor. 8:12-13). It is never implied that the net amount of individual gifts must be the same. This would be as unfair as it would be impractical. Grace giving is not a matter of equal ability to give but it is a matter of equal willingness to give sacrificially, whatever the net amount.

The secret of such giving is the freedom of such giving: "They gave of their own freewill" (2 Cor. 8:3). Just as the great Old Testament passages emphasized giving as one's own heart moved, so the New Testament underscores the radical significance of giving motivated by nothing more than one's own free will. A gift of compulsion is an oxymoron. Giving is not giving when it is coerced. Giving under fear, threat, manipulation, or legalism is not the giving God desires. The secret of such giving is found in the statement, "And not only as we hoped, but they first gave themselves to the Lord, and then to us by the will of God" (2 Cor. 8:5). The order of giving is significant. When personality and life have been given to God, the giving of substance follows as naturally as a rose gives fragrance or the sunlight gives warmth. Failure to give is never a matter of the pocketbook. It is a matter of the heart. When God has us, God will have ours.

Systematic and Biblical Theology
in Light of Stewardship

Every aspect of theological knowledge illuminates every other. One can choose any place to stand within the traditional divisions of systematic theology and find all other divisions illumined in a new way. For example, the Church can be examined in light of God, Christ, Holy Spirit, soteriology, or eschatology. Like holding up a faceted diamond to various angles of light, the Church will be seen in different aspects depending upon the vantage point.

Seldom have the classical divisions of Christian theology been examined in broad outline from the vantage point of stewardship. Stewardship has tended to be an afterthought in any theological system. Yet the doctrines of the Christian faith are illumined and reflect back when examined on the basis of stewardship.

THE DOCTRINE OF GOD

Theology as the doctrine of God always treats that God is and what God is. In a sense, stewardship embraces the question how God relates to us in being-with-God. Humans as humans have a religious consciousness. The awareness of God is not confined to one culture or generation. Even the unbeliever substitutes some other source of ultimate concern for God. Ironically, the atheist cannot leave God alone. Atheists are usually militant about their unbelief. Why has Madilyn Murray O'Hare spent a lifetime fighting what she considers a nonexistent entity? There are good reasons for believing in the universal belief in God.

God is necessary to explain the existence of the world. This is of profound implication for stewardship. Without the existence of God, there is no God to whom we are to be stewards. The very concept of stewardship is impossible without a God to whom we are accountable. To the biblical writers, nature bears witness to God: "The heavens declare the glory of God; and the firmament showeth His handiwork" (Ps. 19:1). If God exists, and if humans are stewards under God, there must be an object of stewardship—the creation in which they live and for which they have an accountability to God as God's stewards.

Further, the world as an object of stewardship is knowable. Something in the minds of humans responds to a pattern in the world. For example, if a chicken leaves marks on a piece of paper, humans cannot decipher those marks. Yet with the discovery of Assyrian cuneiform writing and the deciphering of the Tel-el-Amarna tablets, human minds in the nineteenth century were able to understand exactly what human minds in the eighth century BC meant.

How do humans get meaning out of the world? Humans do not impress meaning onto the world. They find meaning in the world. Meaning implies mind. Mind implies God. God implies our stewardship. The nexus of these concepts requires the existence of God.

Humans hunger for knowledge and truth. Part of human distinctness in the world is the desire to know the world. The search for knowledge and truth has taken humans to the depths below in the bathysphere, to stand on the moon, and send probes into deep space. Whence comes this drive to know? The Earth must be known in order for humans to practice a stewardship of the Earth. An unknown Earth cannot be the object of a rational stewardship. To be a steward of the environment, for example, means that we must know the environment of which we are the stewards.

God is necessary to explain the sense of right and wrong. Inherent in humanity is a sense of oughtness, of differentiation between the morally good and morally bad. This includes the oughtness of stewardship, the sense that I owe to God that which should be given to God.

God is necessary to explain the presence of human will. Humans have the power to achieve, to initiate, to reach goals. No other creation has that volition. If humans are merely a fortuitous collection of atoms and created by impersonal force, then personality has risen above its maker. The lack of stewardship is a will to power that exploits the gifts of God. Stewardship is a will to be accountable for the use of that which God has given. The presence of will in humans implies a Creator and the possibility of stewardship.

Humans are "incurably religious." The rationalist, logical positivist, nihilist, and secularist confidently proclaimed that this century would see the end of the Christian faith. The latest polls show a return to spirituality and near record church attendance in America. How do you account for this thrust toward the unseen, the spiritual, the transcendent? If there is no objective reference—no God—then there is no real reason for religious sentiment, and hence, stewardship.

All of these arguments for the existence of God move from effect to cause. The principle of causality implies that every effect must have a cause. The existence of the universe, rational nature in humans, moral life in a moral order, volitional life, and religious life all imply the existence of God. These arguments can be taken a step further. There is in the human heart a sense of oughtness or responsibility at the point of stewardship. This occurs in every area of life. Humans feel a responsibility for what they do with their time, talents, and treasure. Of course, there are those who have no such feelings whatsoever. But the exception proves the rule. By far most humans have lived and do live with a sense of accountability for what they do with the stuff of life. Whence comes this sense of accountability? Is it an accident? Is it an invention? The burden of stewardship is heavily felt. Many would as soon as not be rid of it. Someone has said, "Whom the gods would curse they first call promising." The awesome weight of unrealized potential lies deep within the human psyche. Animals might be frustrated when they do not achieve what they wish to achieve immediately, but they do not live with a haunting sense of missed destiny because of lost stewardship of life. If every effect has a cause, then God must be the explanation for this unbending sense of oughtness, of accountability as a steward of the stuff of life.

How do the attributes of God relate to Christians as stewards? Each attribute of God has an implication for life as a steward in the creation of God. Foremost, God is personal. This analogous language means that God is more like person than anything else we know. God is certainly more like person than like electricity or gravity. This does not mean that God is merely a projection of our need for a father image. God is not like a person in every way, but is more like a person than like any other kind of existence. Stewardship requires a personal I-Thou sense of human existence. I cannot be a steward in relationship to a machine or a force. There is no sense of necessity to report to, answer to, or sense the judgment of a thing. That God is personal responds to our sense of personal stewardship. If the marks of personality are intelligent, purposive moral life, then God is a perfect personality. We are candidates for personality, growing toward it as it exists in God.

If God is not a person, then no category of the Christian life has any real meaning. Sin is against a person, we repent toward a person, faith is trust in a person, prayer is communion with a person. But also stewardship makes sense only in terms of the personal nature of God. Stewards are stewards toward persons. I owe the electric company; I do not owe electricity. I owe the oil company; I do not owe the gasoline. In some final analysis, every oughtness in life is directed toward a person, not a thing. The personhood of God implies the possibility of stewardship.

The Bible affirms that God is Spirit (John 4:24). This primarily means that God is alive, dynamic, living, and acting. The fact that God is Spirit should not be contrasted to God as material. The negation that God is immaterial falls short of saying what is meant when the church calls God "Spirit." Indeed, it belongs to the Greek or Hellenistic world to insist on pure spirit as the opposite of material. One of the reasons the church might fall short of responsibility in the material world is the insistence that God is not material. Indeed, God is not material, but that negation does not imply God's indifference to or lack

of immanence in the material world. God is extremely concerned with the materiality of the created world. That concern
is a basis for the Christian sense of stewardship in the world.

God is absolute. God does not need anything outside God
in order to exist. This does not mean that God is disconnected
from the created world and hence stewardship. It does mean
that God does not need anything beyond God's own nature in
order to be. God is self-existent. In God is life (John 1:4). That
means that stewardship is not giving to God anything that God
has to have. In primitive religious conceptions—and in some
distortions of the Christian faith—God requires stewardship
because God has need of what humans bring God. In no sense
does God need the gifts humans bring. God is self-existent and
altogether the ground of God's own being.

Part of God's absoluteness is God's oneness or unity. There
is one God and that God is supreme, undivided, and a unity
within Trinity. For stewardship a most important corollary of
this is that the unity of God means the unity of the world. In
principle the world is one. Every part of the world is related to
every other part of the world. This is a major implication for
stewardship. A God who is one and a world that is one implies
a unity and integrity of stewardship in that world. This implies
that individual life is a unity under God: work, home, recreation, church, community, and human physical life are all part
of one greater unity under God. It was noted in chapter 1 that
a disunified view of God in polytheism makes stewardship
impossible. When God is carved up into little pieces with water
gods, Earth goddesses, home idols, and forest fetishes, there can
be no sense of unified stewardship. Time, talent, and treasure
are divided up among a host of demigods with no assurance that

any of them is satisfied. When God is one and life is one, stewardship becomes a possibility in a unified life.

God's omnipresence means that God is everywhere present in the world order. God's omniscience means that God absolutely knows the world order. There is no part of the world order that is not available to the knowledge of God. God's omnipotence means that God's power within the world order is limited only by the nature of God; God cannot contradict God. These attributes of God imply a God who knows our stewardship of life intimately and directly. God is always and everywhere present where we face stewardship decisions. God's power does not coerce us to be stewards. God gives humans the freedom to choose stewardship, not the tyranny to have no choice. There would be no stewardship if humans were fated to give to God.

God is holy, righteous love. These attributes within God do not contradict one another. As holy, God sanctifies all that God touches. This makes the world, time, and personality potentially holy as God is holy. Stewardship treats that which belongs to God as holy because God is holy. God's righteousness is not a static attribute. The righteousness of God means God's activity in making things right. When Christians participate in stewardship, they are making right the use of a fallen material world. God's love expresses itself in giving (John 3:16). God's personal love originated in the Trinity wherein the Persons of the Trinity expressed that love to one another. God gave the Son to the world, the Holy Spirit gave witness to the Son, and the Father and the Son gave the Holy Spirit to the world. The love of God in its very Trinitarian center is a love that gives. The human sense of stewardship originates in that original sense of giving.

How a religion images God determines everything about that faith. Anywhere you approach the doctrine of God you find a God who calls us to be stewards by God's very nature. God is the essence and ideal of loving, responsible personhood. God expressed that personhood in giving. God expressed it in creation and is expressing it in redemption. Stewardship is an essential response to the nature of God.

THE DOCTRINE OF CHRIST

The major considerations of the person and work of Christ have profound implications when viewed from the point of stewardship. Orthodox, historical Christianity in the New Testament, the creeds, and the great dogmaticians have always accepted both the humanity and deity of Jesus Christ. For the purposes of stewardship, it is best to begin with His humanity.

If Jesus Christ were truly man among men, then He lived a life of stewardship on the human level. In the Incarnation, the divine entered the human arena. As in all other areas of human life, Jesus would have been a perfect steward.

Jesus was born. Unlike the Greek demigods or *theos anēr*, He was born after a normal gestation period. Even though His conception was miraculous, His birth was normal human birth. His human mother and supposed father Joseph recognized that birth with the normal act of stewardship at the Temple (Luke 2:22-24). At age twelve, the boy Jesus went to the Passover feast with His parents. At that tender age, He spent three days listening and asking questions of the teachers in the Temple (Luke 2:41-52). He was possessed of an extraordinary insight into questions of faith. He exercised the stewardship of that gift in a dialogue with the religious teachers of the nation. At that point, He acknowledged the first indication of his messianic consciousness: "Did you not know that I must be about My Father's business?" (Luke 2:49). What is this other than a stewardship of life and time for the purposes God intended? We can say that from the very beginning Jesus lived with a sense of stewardship. He acknowledged that stewardship next in submission to His parents (Luke 2:51). What is the stewardship of a child other than in submission to parents?

The summary statement of Luke, "Jesus increased in wisdom and stature, and in favor with God and men" (Luke 2:52) shows the growth in stewardship of life characterizing the silent years of His life. The word *proskopto*, increased, indicates one who moved forward with effort. In every arena of life Jesus demonstrated the stewardship that belonged to that arena of life. Mentally, physically, spiritually, and socially, He grew stronger in the seasons of life. This is the epitome of stewardship under God.

No book more than Hebrews emphasizes the humanity of the Lord Jesus, the Great High Priest. He took our nature because He came to save humans (2:14). He feared and learned obedience though He was God's son (5:8). As part of that obedience, Jesus practiced stewardship as a perfect human being. For Jesus to function as Great High Priest He must take upon Himself all of the responsibilities of the High Priest. Surely, that included a commitment to the stewardship expected of God's faithful servants.

Furthermore, Jesus was sinless. This is a bedrock of belief for Christians. He challenged His generation to convict Him of sin (John 8:46). As noted above, the generation of Jesus was the most tithe-conscious generation in human history. Had Jesus failed at the point of appropriate stewardship of money, He would have been the object of universal public scorn as a religious teacher.

Beyond that, it is almost banal to state that Jesus was a steward of time and talent. In the brief span of His thirty-three-year life on Earth, He moved civilization as no other has done. In that short period, He accomplished the work the Father had sent Him to do. There is no hint of wasted time in Jesus' life. Who could question that Jesus used His abilities as a steward? As in all things Jesus is the model and paradigm for Christians. Yet sinlessness is a passive characteristic. Jesus' life demonstrated the presence of a positive goodness. The absence of positive goodness is itself sin.

That Jesus of Nazareth is the Christ, the Son of God, is the confession of the Bible and the Christian creeds (Mark 1:1; John 1:1-14). That Jesus is the only Son of God is the central message of Christianity. As such, Jesus was the embodiment on Earth of the divine will in heaven. All that Jesus said on giving raised the standard of the Old Testament; it never diminished that statement. Indeed, if the Old Testament standards of stewardship were mistaken, Jesus might well have addressed them in the Sermon on the Mount when He gave the six great contrasts between the oral interpretation of the Law and His own interpretation.

Further, the Cross of the God/Man Jesus was the ultimate expression of giving in history. The worth of the gift was infinite. The one who was not subject to death gave Himself to death that He might be the source of life. The Cross stands in contrast to the other philosophies of human existence. Nihilism claims that there is ultimately nothing to believe. Hedonism lives only for pleasure. Stoicism gives up things in order to demonstrate discipline. Idealism minimizes the reality of earthly human existence. Existentialism emphasizes only the reality that is in the moment. Marxism sees life as a class struggle. Darwinism sees life as a biological struggle. Freudianism knows life only as an inner psychic struggle. In the face of all philosophies stands Jesus Christ, whose gospel insists that giving of life is the only way to finding of life. The Cross is the center and symbol of the Christian faith, and it was primarily the place of giving. Other aspects of the Christian faith might have been the symbol. Since the Incarnation was in a manger, the manger might have been the central symbol of the Christian faith. Since Jesus sat in a boat and taught, a boat might have been the symbol of our faith. Since Jesus worked as our Elder Brother wearing the apron and using the tools of a carpenter, a carpenter's apron might have been the symbol of the faith. Yet the symbol of the faith became the mighty act of self-giving, the Cross.

Yet the Incarnation itself was an act of self-giving by a self-limitation. Jesus did not think that equality with God was a thing to be grasped and retained. His very Incarnation was an act of giving. He gave up the position that He held as the eternal *Logos* and came into human flesh. That this was a stewardship of God's redemptive purposes is obvious. The greatest expression of His stewardship, however, can be seen in Jesus' steadfast commitment to His mission. He early became aware of His messianic consciousness. Certainly no later than His baptism, He knew that His way would be that of a suffering servant messiah whose destiny would be the Cross. In the wilderness He was tempted to take the way of a bread messiah and be crowned king or to prostitute the use of His powers in other ways. He continued in the stewardship of His mission. At every other crisis—the Transfiguration, the Great Confession, the arrest, the trials—Jesus maintained the stewardship of the mission. He did not waver from the use of life that God intended for Him.

The Resurrection is the validation of Jesus' person, work, and teaching. If Jesus still lay in the unrelaxed embrace of death, there would be no ultimate validation of His teaching. But since He was declared to be the Son of God with power by the Resurrection (Rom. 1:4), His person, work, and teaching have the highest sanction in history. That is especially true of Jesus' core value, that one finds life by losing it and that it is more blessed to give than to receive.

But the Resurrection does more than that. The Resurrection underscores the ultimate significance of life in time, space, and material. The destiny of Christ and Christians is not an immaterial spiritual existence. There is a real continuity between life in this world and in the world to come. What one does with the stewardship of time, talent, and treasure in this world radically affects what one experiences in the life beyond. As in all things, the Resurrection is the validation of Jesus' teaching about stewardship.

THE DOCTRINE OF THE HOLY SPIRIT

Biblically and in orthodox historic or creedal Christianity, the Holy Spirit is the Third Person of the Divine Trinity. The Holy Spirit proceeds from both the Father and the Son. The Spirit witnesses to Christ, regenerates believers, empowers them, and distributes gifts for Christian service. It is especially in this latter regard that the doctrine of the Spirit touches upon Christian stewardship.

There is a diversity of gifts bestowed by the Holy Spirit. These gifts build up the Body of Christ. Every member has at least one gift. The Holy Spirit is sovereign in the distribution of gifts. As such the Spirit inspires and guides the life of the church in its worship and service, as well as its stewardship. When Paul deals with the gifts of the Spirit, he places the emphasis on the ethical and service gifts over the spectacular or miraculous gifts (1 Cor. 12-14). There are four lists of spiritual gifts in the New Testament (Rom. 12:6-8; 1 Cor. 12:8-10; 12:28-30; Eph. 4:11). In the Romans passage, one of the gifts is a special spiritual gift of giving. It is unlikely that this means the practice of regularly giving tithes and offerings to God's work. The Holy Spirit gives to some an unusual endowment to give with wisdom and care for the work of God. This is most likely that gift exercised in the early post-Pentecost Jerusalem church. It has been noticed with some degree of humor that the more spectacular gifts create the need for seminars, books, and events. There seldom seems to be a great convocation around the gift of giving. Yet as an ethical gift that gift takes precedence over the more spectacular gifts.

The Holy Spirit baptizes (1 Cor. 12:13) and fills (Eph. 5:18) the believer. However a specific community might see these acts, certainly Christians agree that they empower the believer for a Christian lifestyle. The motive to give must at its roots be moved by the Holy Spirit. There is a legalistic stewardship that comes from the letter of the law. That is a joyless, insipid giving of time, talent, and treasure that does little to enrich the life of the giver. When the Spirit of God becomes the wellspring for giving, stewardship moves into another dimension, one of love, joy, and peace within the Christian community.

The very significance that God gave the Spirit as a gift to the church carries with it the significance of the Spirit for stewardship. The given Spirit empowers Christians to give.

THE DOCTRINE OF THE CHURCH

That Jesus Christ came to found an *ekklesia* or assembly of people called out to Him rests in His very words (Matt. 16:18). Jesus' great affirmation, "I will build my church," has known the most abundant fulfillment of any words spoken by any leader in history. When Jesus spoke those words in the rural Galilean highlands the great reality was Rome. The Roman Forum was the center of the known world. Every mile of the empire was measured from the golden milestone in the Forum. Yet today that Forum rests in ruins. The marble city of Augustus is known only to students of the classics. At the same time the church of Jesus Christ embraces more people in more places than at any time in history. History has validated the words of Jesus about the church.

This is no place for a discussion of church government. That the church of Jesus Christ has developed different forms of government stands as a historical fact. What must be emphasized here, however, is the place of stewardship in the life of the church. As soon as the Spirit of God created the church, stewardship became a necessity. In the earliest days of the Pentecostal Church, it was necessary that the fellowship practice stewardship in the care of its members. Inasmuch as the church is a divine and human organism, the church must know the practice of stewardship to exist on Earth. The mission of the church cannot be carried out without the stewardship of the church.

The primary purpose of the church is worship. The Bible knows humans not primarily as *Homo sapiens* (knower) or *Homo faber* (worker) but as *Homo orans* (worshiper). Humans as humans worship. Worship is at the center of the church's existence. The affirmation and praise of God is the wellspring of all else in the church. It should be kept in mind that the Bible knows nothing of a worship of God without a giving to God. In chapter 2 it was noted that the earliest acts of worship were acts of giving. To separate the two is foreign to biblical ideas of worship. That one would come to worship God with empty hands was abhorrent. The belief of some that New Testament worship has nothing equivalent to an offering to God as is the case in the Old Testament worship is wide of the mark. The very center of worship was the act of giving to God.

Out of the worship in the church comes the activities of the church. Service, mission, evangelism, and ethical action spring from the center of worship. The activities of the church in the world are impossible without stewardship of time, talent, and treasure. This is where the theological becomes the practical and the doctrinal becomes the ethical. Because God has met us in worship we must respond with that stewardship of life that underwrites Christian mission. Implicit in Jesus' statement "I will build my church" is the life of stewardship.

In this regard, there is a curious distinction among American church members according to a poll in *The Average American Book* by Barry Tarshis:

- 95 percent say they believe in God;
- 70 percent say they believe in an afterlife;
- 61 percent belong to one of the 250 religious orders or groups in the country;
- 84 percent consider religion an important influence in their lives.

Yet the same poll demonstrated that Americans spend their money in the following percentages:

- 21 percent on food and tobacco;
- 8 percent on clothing;

- 15 percent on housing;
- 14.5 percent on transportation;
- 6.5 percent on recreation;
- 1 percent on religion and welfare.[1]

Such statistics as these indicate that in late-twentieth-century America, doctrine has not translated itself into action. There is a cleavage in the American mind between religious affiliation and stewardship that does not reflect the biblical norm.

No mere tactical or programmatic action will correct this dichotomy. There must be a return to the radical understanding of church as God's people on mission, as that community that exists by mission as fire exists by burning.

THE ANTHROPOLOGICAL ACCOUNTABILITY OF STEWARDSHIP

The predicament of humans in biblical anthropology can be stated in one word: Sin. Sin is that cosmic rebellion against God of which individual sins are the example. The rich vocabulary of the New Testament gives a fully orbed understanding of sin. *Adikia* stands for sin as misdeed. *Hamartia* has often been translated as missing the mark. This is not adequate. It implies that humans were aiming. *Anomia* refers to sin as lawlessness. *Apistia* indicates unfaithfulness, lack of belief, or even disbelief. *Asebeia* names sin as lack of reverence or godlessness. *Aselgeia* marks sin as licentiousness. *Epithumia* describes sin as lust, or an inordinate and unregulated desire for that which is not best. *Echthra* defines sin as hostile feelings or enmity. *Kakia* is one of the strongest feelings for sin as wickedness or depravity. *Parabasis* describes sin as going outside the boundaries of life. *Ponēria* marks sins as maliciousness or baseness.

Sin belongs to the essential human. Sin is not marginal to an otherwise wholesome center of life. Sin has taken the very citadel of humanity. It reigns. It defies remedy. It creates obsessions and compulsions that so drive humans that they know they are destroying themselves but cannot stop. Sin looms as an almost personified force of towering dimensions. The whole of humanity is involved in sin: flesh, spirit, heart, and soul (the principle categories of biblical anthropology). Sin can be described as willfulness, against knowledge, as unbelief, against God as a person, as guilt, depravity, bondage, and an evil heart.

Perhaps sin as depravity relates most comprehensively to human failure in stewardship. Depravity is that state of the human moral nature that makes it not only possible that humans might sin but makes it certain. Such depravity is both inherent and universal. Depravity does not indicate that each individual human is as evil as that person might possibly be. Depravity does mean that sin has touched every area of the human existence; there is no area not touched by sin. Sin invades the marketplace in deceptive trade, the home in divorce, recreational life in such a way that sport becomes malice, art in the aesthetic distortion, and stewardship in the selfish use of time, talent, and treasure. As depravity relates to stewardship is indication that humans use time unwisely, talent for improper ends, and treasure for selfish purposes. This is the universal experience of humans. Humans are totally helpless in the face of the sin factor. Every element of human life has been weakened as a result of sin. Humans are totally unable to deliver themselves from sin. Indeed, left to themselves humans only become worse and worse.

Depravity has touched stewardship at every point. Whatever humans touch in the realm of stewardship they taint. The desire for an honest living through work becomes a driving obsession to make more and more. The use of time becomes a compulsive use of hours for one's own ends. Ability is squandered on selfish purposes rather than godly intentions. Depravity makes every arena of stewardship appear to be slightly askew, like a painting on the wall that does not hang straight. Everything in it is tilted.

Sin is also bondage. It produces a state of slavery from which humans cannot liberate themselves. Romans 6 and 7 speak to sin as bondage. The human might even know the good, but be unable to perform the good. There is an enslaving quality to possessions. Thoreau stated in Walden that the necessities of human existence are food, shelter, and clothes. In that classic of American literature he demonstrated the bondage in which the residents of Concord, Massachusetts, lived in order to have property and be in style. Although the Transcendentalist aspect of Thoreau did not cause him to refer to sin, he painted a picture of sin as bondage to the material rather than stewardship. When stewardship ceases to be a motive in human life, there develops a bondage to things. Luxuries quickly become necessities and life becomes a slavery to provide them. Humans live a treadmill existence of slavery to the material for no rational reason.

THE LANGUAGE OF BIBLICAL THEOLOGY

At the most fundamental level, all theology rests on exegesis. To grasp the concept of steward in all of its biblical nuance, we must examine the very development and use of the word in classical Greek, the LXX, the Hebrew used by the rabbis, the New Testament, and the Fathers. Words are always interpreted by their context and development.

The word was used by Plato, Aeschylus, and Xenophon in the sense of a steward. The word was also used in the papyri and inscriptions. The word could be used as the Greek equivalent for the office of procurator. The word could be used of one in charge of separate branches of a household, inspector of goods, or even chief cook. In each instance it implies someone entrusted with responsibility in the house of another. The word in the LXX and rabbinical writings can be used of a kind of chief slave who superintended the household and even the whole property of his master. It could be used for the child or son of the house. It became a loan word to be used of city officials such as the treasurer. It could be used in the sense of a housekeeper, estate manager, or accountant.[2]

One must understand that the use of this term was "in the air" that provided the atmosphere of New Testament theology. It had already received a religious twist in its use by pious pagan Greeks to point out those who had different responsibilities in the religious cults of Greece. Helge Brattgard, a respected European theologian of stewardship, points out:

> The background for all the Bible says about the steward is found in this, that God in His goodness thinks so highly of the human being that He will trust him to administer that which belongs to God. The steward's calling rests on confidence. But this is not a question of confidence as it is generally considered. What is remarkable about the biblical idea is the fact that the steward has a unique authority. He is a fully authorized representative, free to deal independently on behalf of his master, at the same time that he is completely dependent upon his master. When his stewardship is over he will have to give an account of how he took care of the calling which, as just noted, involves both dependence and independence.[3]

The pertinent points in every biblical story of the *oikonomos* can be found in the story of Eliezer the steward of Abraham

(Gen. 24:1-67). The long and detailed narrative contains within it virtually every dimension of the biblical sense of stewardship. Eliezer was the senior servant or steward in the house of Abraham who ruled over all that he had. As such he would have had responsibility for 318 other attendants as well as an enormous herd of cattle, flock of sheep, etc. His stewardship became specific when Abraham commanded him to find a wife for Isaac. This stewardship was taken under a strong oath (vv. 3-4). He was given specific instructions about what his stewardship was to be and not to be (vv. 5-7). He was further given the circumstances under which he was released from his stewardship (v. 8). His specific act of stewardship was preceded by prayer (v. 12) and followed by worship (v. 26) when he had found a wife for Isaac. As a steward he gave testimony to his master's goodness, greatness, and wealth (v. 35). Finally, he was able to give an account of pursuing his stewardship until it was finally finished.

Joseph, the grandson of Abraham, also gives an excellent model for the meaning of steward in the Old Testament. He was in a sense a man so committed to being a steward that he by temperament could not help being a steward. When Joseph was sold into slavery he became part of Potiphar's household. Potiphar was captain of the Pharaoh's guard (Genesis 39). Potiphar watched the wisdom and personal faith of Joseph. He made Joseph his "overseer," a position of full authority over his house (v. 4). Joseph was such a faithful steward that everything about Potiphar's household and farming prospered (v. 5). The extent of this trust toward a steward is expressed in verse 6: "Thus, he left all that he had in Joseph's hand, and he did not know what he had except for the bread which he ate." When

Potiphar's wife tried to seduce and compromise Joseph, Joseph remained true to his trust. When she falsely accused Joseph and he was imprisoned, he soon became a trustee in the prison in charge of all the prisoners (v. 22). Finally, because of his sagacity, Joseph was made second in all of Egypt under Pharaoh, the stewardship of an entire nation (Gen. 41:40-41). Joseph demonstrates aspects of a faithful steward for all times. He demonstrates that stewardship operates at every level of life. He was a faithful steward over little, so he then became a faithful steward over much. He demonstrates growth as a steward from smaller situations to greater.

In contrast to these faithful stewards stands the case of Shebna (Isa.22:12-23). Shebna was a *sōken*, the Hebrew word for steward. He probably occupied the position of prime minister. Instead of watching over his stewardship, he was preparing for himself a grand tomb. God will intervene to toss Shebna out of his stewardship like tossing a ball into a field (v. 18). He will be replaced with another steward, Eliakim, who will treat his stewardship of Jerusalem like a father to the city (v. 21). There is further introduced here the power of the key. Eliakim will be given the key of the house of David to wear on his shoulder (v. 22). This becomes the image of a steward and is even used of Christ in Rev. 3:7. Eliakim will be of such quality as a steward that he will be like a peg fastened in a secure place (v. 23).

Here we see the abuse and loss of stewardship, as well as the transfer of stewardship to another. This is an Old Testament anticipation of the parable of the talents (Matt. 25:14-30) in which the one who did not use stewardship had his talent taken and given to the faithful steward.

In the New Testament the term *oikonomos* occurs first in the parables of Jesus. In the parable of the faithful steward Jesus speaks of the nature of stewardship (Luke 12:41-48). "Who then is that faithful and wise steward, whom his master will make ruler over his household, to give them their portion of food in due season?" (v. 42). Here are two qualities of the steward set out in the Greek text. The steward is *pistos*, faithful. This is the *sine qua non* of a steward. The steward is also *phronimos*. That term for wisdom indicates particularly the ability to apply wisdom to individual situations, the very essence of a steward's situation. Jesus then pronounces His *makarios* (blessing) on a steward who acts with faith and wisdom in his master's absence. When the master suddenly returns and finds the steward faithful he will reward him with even more stewardship (v. 44). In contrast to this is the faithless, imprudent steward who takes advantage of his master's absence. He abuses the others of the household and indulges himself in food and drink. He will be surprised by his master's return, cut in two, beaten, and have his portion with infidels.

In this and similar instances the words *oikonomos* and *doulos* are used interchangeably. This shows that the *oikonomos* is a steward from among the slaves who is over the whole household and sometimes the whole property of his master. The opposite of this case is in Luke 16:1-13, where the *oikonomos* is a free treasurer who abused his position of trust.

An *oikonomos* could even be the treasurer of the city. In Paul's concluding remarks to the Romans he joins with him in the greetings, "Erastus, the *oikonomos* of the city" (Rom. 16:23). The city in question was Corinth, from which Paul wrote the Roman letter. Stewardship could be of such magnitude that it included an entire city in the secular sense of a steward.

Another aspect of the terms *oikonomos* is found in Gal. 4:1-2. The son and heir of a family is under guardians (*epitropoi*) and stewards (*oikonomoi*). Here one word seems to define the other. It is part of the task of the guardian to supervise the support and education of minors, but also to administer the whole inheritance to their benefit and advantage. In the popular mind the guardian and the steward were one and the same.

In 1 Cor. 4:1 Paul wishes that he and the apostles be regarded "as servants of Christ and *oikonomoi* of the mysteries of God." Here stewardship embraces the apostolic responsibility to declare the musterion of God, that which was not known before Christ but now fully revealed in him. 1 Cor. 4:2 once again announces that the chief qualification of a steward is faithfulness (cf. Luke 12:42; 16:10-11; Matt. 25:21, 23).

Oikonomos came to have a place in the common legacy of the primitive Christian tradition. In Titus 1:7 we are told "a bishop must be blameless, as an *oikonomos* of God." This bishop as a steward of the gospel is to live a life consonant with that responsibility. 1 Pet. 4:10 broadens stewardship to make every believer a steward of the manifold grace of God. 1 Pet. 4:11 indicates that office bearers particularly are stewards of God.

An example of the early patristic use is found in Ignatius: "Labor together, fight, run, suffer, sleep, watch with one another as God's stewards, companions, and servants" (*oikonomoi, paredroi, hupéretai*). Here stewardship is joined with exertion, vigilance, and the shared life of the Christian community. Philo speaks of a wise man who is both *polutikos kai oikonomos* (we would say "statesman and steward"): "Because the wise man merits praise in all his movements and in all situations, in the house and outside, as statesman and ruler of the house, because he rules well in the house and acts in a statesmanlike way out-side, as is beneficial to the improvement of society." Here the steward is one worthy of approbation in every situation and context, both in the private life of the home and in the public life of the community.

From this review of Greek, Hebrew, New Testament, and patristic usage, what can be summarized about the office of a steward? A steward is entrusted with responsibility in the house of another. The steward is extended the confidence of the owner and acts with independence. The steward might be given a specific task of significance within that overall stewardship (Eliezer). The steward observes his stewardship with prayer and worship. From Joseph we see that stewardship by its nature grows from smaller arenas to larger, from stewardship of the less to the greater. A steward is wise and faithful. The steward might have to give a sudden accounting of his stewardship at any time. A steward's position is not unlike that of a guardian for a child, looking after everything for the advantage of the child. The object of stewardship for a Christian might be something intangible, the mysteries of the gospel. The steward is to exer-cise stewardship in all contexts, both private and public.

Oikonomia

Just as *oikonomos* refers to the steward, the *oikonomia* is the office the steward holds, the stewardship. In Greek from the time of Xenophon and Plato, *oikonomia* describes the office held by the steward. The word can apply to household admin-istration, direction, provision, and could be used for example of a prefect settling men in their homeland. Josephus uses the term of Pharoah charging Joseph with the *oikonomia*, the whole execution of the matter. The word can be traced in classical Greek from management of a household to the administration of an entire state. The word group came by degrees to be used in a broader context. In medicine, for example, the word came to be used for the care of the body. Finally, the word came to have the sense of the administration of the universe in a religious sense.

The word is used in the LXX two times, the New Testament nine times, and the apostolic fathers six times. The New Testament use of the word includes the office of household administrator and the discharge of that office (Luke 16:2ff). Paul uses the word of his apostolic office. He has been entrusted with an *oikonomian* (1 Cor. 9:17). The word is so used in the prison letters. Paul has an *oikonomian* toward the Colossians which God had given him (Col. 1:25). Paul has been given an *oikonomian* or office of grace laid upon him by God for the Ephesians (Eph. 3:2). It is most instructive that in the prison letters it is difficult to tell whether the phrase is used in the sense of a stewardship by Paul or the stewardship of the plan of salvation that belongs to God. This very ambiguity is instructive. The stewardship might be that of God in God's administration of the plan of salvation, or it might be that of Paul in the administration of his apostolic office. The two blend together in the latter New Testament (Eph. 1:10; 3:9). To be involved with God as a stewardship is to be involved in a stewardship of the very plan of salvation, as well as the administration of one's own particular part of that plan.

Chapter Seven

The Stewardship of Creation

Since the first "Earth Day" in 1970, the news media, academia, sciences, and theologies have continued a heated debate on the nature, extent, and cause of the ecological crisis. Some Christians have considered the threats of the ecological crisis as a sign of the "last days." Others have denied its existence. Still others have joined the ranks of environmentalists, calling for a theological perspective on the ecological crisis.

Our generation has been the first in history to see the planet Earth from outside. Astronomer Fred Hoyle made the striking assertion, "Once a photograph of the Earth, taken from the outside is available... a new idea as powerful as any in history will be let loose."[1] Virtually all of the one hundred or more astronauts from various countries and religions have reported their awe at the sight of the whole Earth—"its beauty, fertility, smallness in the abyss of space, light and warmth under the sun in surrounding darkness and, above all, its vulnerability."[2]

IS THERE AN ECOLOGICAL DISASTER?

Ethicist Ebbie C. Smith has recently addressed the existence and extent of the ecological crisis.[3] Is there indeed a crisis, or has humanity been subjected to the constant and meaningless threats of alarmists? Roger L. DiSilvestro says humanity "stands in the shadow of global catastrophe." Ian G. Barbour warns that pollution of rivers, soil, and air are exterminating species and using up world resources.

On the other hand, there are those who claim that the alarm is a hoax. Gregg Easterbrook states that since the first Earth Day in 1970, most measures of United States ecology have improved. Industrial pollution is down, the Great Lakes are recovering from the chemical infested soup they had become, and things are generally improving. He states that the environment can reverse itself and heal itself quickly.

Dixie Lee Ray, a former governor of Washington and chair of the Atomic Energy Commission, insists that humans have a minimum rather than maximum impact on the ecosystem. In her view, the Earth has received much worse insults from earlier generations and has recovered.

Most radically, Edward C. Krug, a soil scientist, sees the entire crisis as a hoax of scare tactics. The environmentalists, in his view, want to destroy the free enterprise system and place the burden of an intolerable debt on the American people to clean up what does not need to be cleaned.

On the other hand, Anglican intellectual and clergyman John Stott considers the ecocrisis to be the greatest peril. Human covetousness has spoiled the Earth. Twenty years before most evangelicals recognized the crisis, the late Frances Schaffer pointed out the looming threat and the need for

Christian action. The evidence can be listed selectively: The cutting of mountain forests in Tibet, Nepal, Bhutan, and Northern India results in devastation by monsoon rains causing floods rather than renewing the topsoil. Fifteen acres per year are becoming desert in Asia, Africa, and Latin America. Rain forest destruction in the Amazon has actually been subsidized by government. African population growth and land destruction since 1967 has resulted in a 20 percent drop in grain production, a disaster. In developed nations 65 percent of grain is fed to livestock in contrast to 16 percent in underdeveloped nations. The movement of the Sahara into Africa is now measured in miles per year.

William A. Dryness reports seeing the devastation as Kikuyu women in Kenya harvest firewood in order to cook. They walk for hours each day in order to find firewood to cook for their families. From the air, one can see giant barren circles around villages where the women have cleared the firewood for cooking fuel. This illustrates the struggle between basic survival of human life on the one hand and ecosystems on the other. Meanwhile, our 8 percent of the population uses 40 percent of the Earth's resources.[4]

NEW RELIGIONS EMERGING FROM THE ECOLOGICAL DEBATE

Moral philosophers such as Holmes Rolston III have contended that nature and animals do not have "rights" in the same sense that humans have rights. Since such a basis in natural law has been removed philosophically from the ecosystem, what can be a final, transcendent motivation for the care of planet Earth? Many realize that the environmental movement cannot sustain its own passion without some ultimate ontological reference. One answer has been the "deep ecology" movement. This movement approaches a religious consciousness as motive for the environment. Bill DeVall and George Sessions state:

> Deep ecology goes beyond the so-called factual, scientific level to the level of self and Earth wisdom… [It] goes beyond a limited, piecemeal shallow approach to environmental problems and attempts to articulate a comprehensive religious and philosophical worldview. The foundations of deep ecology are the basic intuitions and experiencing of ourselves and Nature which comprise ecological consciousness… Many of these questions are perennial philosophical and religious questions faced by humans in all cultures over the ages.[5]

Further, the loss of self deprives one of any vehicle for stewardship. There is no self to be responsible for life in the world. The loss of individual existence renders the very concept of stewardship void of meaning. If one does not have a conscious over-againstness in contrast to the universe, there is no self to hold responsible for the environment. The environmental movement is not one of "self-less" people who have no sense of individual existence.

It is highly unlikely that those who espouse the Buddhist philosophy as the cure for American environmental ills would go so far as to surrender the other benefits of Western civilization: mobility, the Internet and World Wide Web, the certainty of food on their plates, or the university educations that were a result of the Western Judeo-Christian environment. Those who live under the passive state created by the Hindu or Buddhist philosophies do not have the leisure to consider the recondite questions of world stewardship.

Without being politically incorrect, it is a fact that concern for the world environment has found its most vocal expression in those cultures that are the fruit of the Judeo-Christian tradition. It would seem that Hindu, Buddhist, or Taoist cultures would have produced most concern for the environment if basis for such concern is indeed rooted in those worldviews. There is no evidence that the loss of self leads to a renewed concern for the world environment.

OLD PAGAN ROOTS FOR EARTH-FRIENDLY RELIGIONS

Ecofeminism reflects a term coined in 1974 by French writer Francois d'Eaubonne. As the title suggests, the movement considers the exploitation of nature a reflection of a patriarchal Judeo-Christian tradition. Nature is universally spoken of as feminine in all languages. "Mother Nature" is the term by which the world is often designated. On the other hand, such phrases as "man against nature" demonstrate a male hostility to the nurture of nature. Hurricanes were traditionally called by female names. There is the suggestion that there is something in nature akin to man's perception of woman: mysterious, beautiful, dangerous, and tempting. The feminists have connected the witch trials in which the Salem witches were persecuted to the attitudes of human males toward nature.

Of course, in this tradition the patriarchal religion of the Bible with a Father God and a male Lord and Savior comes in for criticism. The ecofeminists call for a return to a religion dominated by a female nature goddess in which there was no war and confrontation but a nurturing relationship of equality between men and women. Such a religion would therefore be environmentally friendly and lead to a renewed understanding and friendship with and in the ecosystem.

One cannot be unfriendly to the core of concern in this argument. A strictly male image of God has led to a misunderstanding of the nature of both God and what it is to be fully human. The concerns of women cannot be ignored in any dimension of human life today. Yet there is at the same time no definite, historical laboratory in which to test the thesis that women are per se more friendly toward the environment than are men.

Other Religious Alternatives for Ecological Motivation

Monism is a philosophical term indicating the belief that everything is ultimately one, that all existence belongs to one greater existence. This has found its place in the Western writings of Benedict de Spinoza as well as Eastern religions. The basic thesis of monism finds its support in the interrelatedness of life and nature. At the heart of human existence are molecules consisting largely of carbon, a basic element in the universe. The algae in water creates oxygen. In turn humans inhale oxygen and exhale carbon dioxide. Plants absorb the carbon dioxide in photosynthesis. Everyone on the planet has breathed at least one molecule of oxygen that Jesus Christ breathed. There is a great continuity of oneness in the natural world.

From such observations as this come varieties of expression of a one-world soul, a unified existence in which the whole is more than the sum of its parts. Ecologists consider this view significant to provide a religion for their ideology. They suspect, rightly, that mere humanistic passion cannot sustain a crusade of the dimensions they imagine necessary. Consequently, there must be some transcendent motive, a spiritual coefficient of the battle to save the Earth.

The foil to this is Christianity. The Christian view that God created a universe which God stands over against, that humankind is separate from nature, and the role of humans is to have dominion over nature is the essence of evil to the monist ecologist. That we are part of nature, one great world soul, should imply a care for the world's environment. In this view, the Judeo-Christian movement has interfered with the natural order of things.

Insurmountable difficulties exist with this view. As with all such postulates, it cannot prove itself on the basis of its own epistemology. If all existence is one, how could the perverse idea ever have arisen that it is not! The system would have risen above itself. The monistic universe could hardly produce a distortion that would challenge its own existence.

Further, monism leaves no place for individual responsibility in the face of ecology. Each nonindividual thus by his or her very nature should go with the flow of preserving the environment. Yet today we find individuals in developed and underdeveloped, Eastern and Western, literate and illiterate cultures who are equally destructive of the environment.

By the philosophical dictum of "the most likely explanation," the biblical account makes the most sense. There is a Creator God whose creation was perfection. In that Edenic paradise, there was a oneness of Adam and Eve with the Garden environment. They were not identified with the Garden. They were in it but different from it. The Garden was their responsibility. When they rebelled against God, it changed them, the Garden, and their attitude toward the Garden. They are now outside the Garden. The Garden resists them and they exploit the Garden. This accounts for the world as we see it far more plausibly than the monist view of identity with the world.

The Gaia hypothesis was a term coined by scientist James Lovelock in 1975. The Greek word *gaia* is that word referring to the Earth or nature. It recalls the early feminine terms of "Mother Earth." In conjunction with the ecofeminism movement, it emphasizes the feminine aspect of nature. Lovelock conducted research examining the Earth's environment in comparison with the supposed environment of Mars:

> It appeared to us that the Earth's biosphere is able to control at least the temperature of the Earth's surface and the composition of the atmosphere. *Prima facie*, the atmosphere looked like a contrivance put together by the totality of living systems to carry out certain control functions. This led to the proposition that living matter, the air, the oceans, the land surface, were parts of a giant system which was able to control temperature, the composition of the air and sea, the pH of soil and so on as to be optimal for survival of the biosphere. The system seemed to exhibit the behavior of a single organism, even a living creature.[6]

Lovelock's observation, little more than an analogy, has been expanded by others into a near religion. In this viewpoint, the universe has in a sense continued to create itself. In the aggregate, it has a mind and reason that it does not demonstrate in the particular. By analogy one might come to the conclusion that the human hand must have created the human body because the body is such a wonderful appendage to the hand. Nature has risen above itself in the Gaia hypothesis.

If one found a watch in the Sahara Desert, one would not first say, "How wonderful that the aggregate of all the desert sand dreamed up, designed, created, and sustained this watch." You would likely posit a watchmaker somewhere who made the watch and then lost it in the desert. When such arguments about the macrocosm as the Gaia hypothesis are reduced to the level of the microcosm, their fallacy is exposed. Ecologists are right in wanting a religious impulse to sustain their concern; they look for it in an insufficient source in the Gaia hypothesis.

Further, if this were true in the larger units of the ecosystem, it should be observable in every smaller unit. There should be evidence that subunits of nature produce their own sustenance. This is not the case.

The New Physics has produced a new type of environmental religion. The New Physics is not all that new. The work on which it is based took place in the earlier part of the twentieth century. Einstein's Theory of Relativity theorized that time, space, and mass were all relative to one's vantage point. One can make time slow down, space shrink, and mass reduce itself, depending upon the vantage point from which one looks. If one could travel at the speed of light—186,000 miles per second— time would slow to nothing, etc. This view destroyed the ordered world of Newtonian physics, the clockwork universe which worked in perfect, predictable order. If time, space, and mass depended on one's vantage point, there was an uncertainty introduced into the natural scheme of things which could not be explained. In a new sense the mysterious entered into the natural world.

Then entered Heisenberg with his principle of indeterminancy. According to quantum physics, one cannot at the same time determine the speed and location of a subatomic particle. The very act of attempting to measure this upsets the equation. At the subatomic level, things happen unpredictably, in an indeterminate way. At the heart of matter is not predictability, but an unpredictable random action.

To make this as a scientific observation is one thing. To base a religious worldview on it is another. Physicist Fritjof Capra has extrapolated from the New Physics a worldview:

> Relativity theory has made the cosmic web come alive, so to speak, by revealing its essentially dynamic character; by showing that its activity is the very essence of its being. In modern physics, the image of the universe as a machine has been transcended by a view of it as one indivisible dynamic whole whose parts are essentially interrelated and can be understood only as patterns of a cosmic process. At the subatomic level, the interrelations and interactions between the parts of the whole are more fundamental than the parts themselves. There is motion but there are, ultimately, no moving objects; there is activity, but there are no actors; there are no dancers, there is only the dance.[7]

Once again, you have a system that has risen above itself. Inanimate nature has created mind. The mind-brain relationship has never been solved. How the reality of thought relates to the physical construction of the human brain has never been determined by neurologists or philosophers. Yet when considering the relationship between the human brain and thought, one can at least understand that there are physical neurons along which electrical charges travel in the creation of thought. To posit that totally disconnected entities in the universe are somehow interacting with one another absent any physical connection—by some mysterious ether?—takes more faith than the Christian faith. The New Physics cannot provide a sustaining basis for the stewardship of the ecosystem.

The oriental religions have likewise pressed their claims as a belief system capable of sustaining the ecological crusade. Hinduism, Taoism, and Buddhism all have at their hearts the denial of the individual existence. In these religions the self is absorbed into a greater reality. The goal is the loss of all individual existence into the great whole of the universe. This is, of course, the exact opposite of the Christian view of the resurrection of the body at the last day. While the Christian hopes for such a resurrection and continuation of individual existence, the Hindu or Buddhist looks at this idea with horror. The goal for them is the cessation of consciousness, since existence is equated with suffering.

Seizing this central tenant of the East—the loss of self—some have proffered the Eastern religions as the suitable basis to sustain the ecological movement. The argument falls along several lines. Since Christianity values the individual self, it pushes the self ahead of the whole. It is the self-conscious, achieving, developing, exploiting individual that destroys the environment. Lose that sense of individuality, and all will be well with nature.

If this were true, one would suspect certain things that are not so. India would be a nation phenomenally concerned with its own environment. Visit Calcutta or Bangalore and you will quickly see that this is not the case. Cows roam the airport parking lots and wallow in their own dung. Village women brush their teeth with the same cow dung. Infants die in shocking numbers. Villages are decimated with leprosy and typhoid fever. If this were true, the Buddhists of China would have created a nation consumed with the preservation of the environment. One would have to be miserably uninformed to consider China the center of the environmental movement. If the Eastern religions were sustaining a stewardship of the environment, they should be doing so in the very place of their highest concentration. Exactly the opposite is the case.

The center of environmental concern is the United States, whose entire educational system is predicated on values of the

Judeo-Christian movement. There would be no empirical science as we know it without the Western tradition. Only the most perverse revisionism of history on a university campus gone mad with the denial of the obvious could deny that modern science arose in Western civilization. The empirical method on which all science is based did not arise in Hindu countries. It arose in a culture where self was separate from the thing being studied. The very chemical tests that allow ecologists to declare the disaster are possible because of a Western culture that sees the self separate from the nature that self studies.

Inadequacy of Monistic and Pagan Models

The models above cannot sustain the religious motivation needed for a stewardship of creation. Stewardship is rigorous business. It cannot sustain itself on a diet of spiritual vapor. One can look with awe at the religious traditions of the Orient. Yet the Christian must measure them against the vastly different message of the Lord Jesus Christ. The religio-philosophical systems of Gaia, New Physics, ecofeminism, or regionalism are such novelties in the historical continuum that no one could seriously contend that they have stood the test of time necessary to sustain the human exertion implied in the ecological struggle. If the fight to save the planet endures, it must have that kind of power implied in the Resurrection of the Lord Jesus Christ, Pentecost, and ethical impulse of historic Christian faith.

THE NATURE OF BEING AS CHRISTIAN STEWARDS

Before the particulars of a Christian stewardship of the planet, one must stand back to ask the question, "How do Christians exist in relationship to otherness?" If we are stewards, how do we relate to that for which we are stewards?

Douglas John Hall has written cogently of the nature of human existence within the possibilities of stewardship. His thought can best be introduced with a graphic illustration of the three dimensions of relatedness toward God, humanity, and the natural world. These dimensions of existence are not independent of one another. They flow from one another and necessarily imply one another:

Essential (intended or authentic) humanity means:

being-with (coexistence)

=being-for (proexistence)

=being-together (communion, community, covenant)

Existential (distorted, inauthentic, "fallen" humanity means:

being-alone (autonomy)

=being-against (estrangement, alienation)

=being-above (pride = the attempt at mastery) or

being-below (sloth = escape from responsibility)[8]

To understand the stewardship of creation in its most general terms, we must understand these three dimensions of creation. We are created to be with God, to be with one another, and to be with the natural world. Christian theology has concentrated on the former two, but not as much on the last— being with nature. In the Western tradition there have been two ways of looking at the stewardship of nature: man subsumed under nature or nature subsumed under man. Yet in some instinctive way, biblical people understand that neither is the actual case. Humans are not under the power of nature, yet nature is not under the power of humans.

That humans are "above" nature in the Western tradition is really not strong enough. The phrase which better images our stewardship of nature is the phrase "conquering nature." Humanity sees itself in a war to overcome, subdue, and conquer the natural world. Metaphor is powerful. Why has the Western world, up to the 1960s, spoken positively of "conquering nature," rather than being for nature as stewards? When one looks at the icons of modern urban living, one sees everywhere the intention to control nature. In the perfectly manicured lawns of suburbia, there is the control of grasses and shrubs. In the captivity of whales at marine parks, there is the desire to control the whale and life of the sea. In the 2,250 head of cattle eaten daily in McDonald's hamburgers there is the desire to control domestic cattle. Without any question there is a will to dominate, to control, and to use nature thus conquered. Yet is this being above nature what God intended in God's command that we have dominion over nature?

Does this desire to control nature not root in our own sense of fear, helplessness, and estrangement from the natural world? We see nature as other, as threat, as that which must be contained or it will overcome us. This is the curse of Eden, the alienation from their environment that Adam and Eve felt when they were expelled into the blasted and cursed Earth outside the gates. The exploitation of and lack of stewardship toward the natural world in the industrial and postindustrial world demands more explanation than Yankee ingenuity, the desire to get ahead, or the progress of humanity. There is throughout the process the desire to control, to dominate beyond the necessary. It becomes not only a being-above but also a being-against.

In Nature and Different from Nature

Part of any understanding of stewardship by humans of the non-human natural world must address the tension of our relationship with nature. We are Adam (Heb. *'ādām* = "man," "people") from Adamah (Heb. *'ădāmāh* = "ground"), human from the humus. We are from the dust and go to the dust. We are part of the natural process. We are in nature just as every other created thing. Yet at the same time we live with the consciousness unknown in any other part of creation—we know that we are different from other creatures. Adam alone names the creatures in the Garden. Adam alone knows aspiration, guilt, shame, and alienation from God. To put it another way, you have many concerns that your dog cannot, does not, and never will have. Unless you are an unusual devotee of the canine, you understand that your dog does not reflect on "dogness," what makes "dogness" different from "catness," and the origin and destiny of all dogs. Only humans reflect on those questions. That sets us apart from nature.

Indeed, the very possibility of stewardship roots in that difference. Your dog does not worry about stewardship of the backyard. In contrast with the new religions proposed by some ecologists, unless we are distinct from nature we cannot have a concern for nature called stewardship. There is today great pressure on Christian theologians to discard the transcendent aspect of our stewardship and replace it with a total identification with nature as stewards. If we are indeed transcendent and have dominion over nature (a term out of favor with the ecologists), what is the nature of that dominion? Hall suggests that we reimage our dominion in terms of a vocational relationship to nature. We are "assigned" a role in nature. Rather than the older Western tradition, which vaunts the superiority of humans to the degree that the rest of the world is only a stage for their prima donna performance, we simply have a different job to do in the natural order created by God. We must

181

understand that humans are different in more than one dimension. Humans also created Auschwitz and Belsen. Humans produced a Stalin and Hitler. That difference is one of tragic proportions to bless or to blast.

Any adequate understanding of human stewardship must see humans as both in nature and beyond nature, participating and yet different. For the Christian steward, all things must be settled Christologically. What was the nature of being-as-a-steward reflected in the Lord Jesus Christ? Earlier we have viewed the Incarnation as a model of stewardship. In Christ, God both entered into the natural world and at the same time transcended the natural world. The Advent at Bethlehem saw the eternal enter the temporal, and in so doing gave the temporal world a significance it would otherwise never have had. It made a sacrament of time and history. It made holy the profession of a carpenter and by implication all other honorable professions. It rent the veil of the Temple and sacralized the world for the believer.

How does the lordship of Christ behave in the world? The great kenotic hymn of Phil. 2:6-10 expresses this lordship in terms that define dominion Christologically. The same Christ who was "in the form of God" was also the Christ who "taking the form of a bondservant...humbled Himself...." The Christian's model of dominion is Christ. It is in Christ that we see dominion exemplified. Christ's lordship is exemplified in His servant-type stewardship. We are accountable to Him to model that same kind of stewardship. It is He who said, "I am among you as One Who serves." We must understand that the being-as-a-servant related not only to God and to other humans, but also to the natural environment.

THE MIRACLES OF A SERVANT—LORD AS A KEY TO STEWARDSHIP

Most New Testament theologians today acknowledge that the miracles of Jesus were not merely acts to provoke blank astonishment. They were making statements about what He intended life to be in His Kingdom. The miracles show the desire of God if the will of God were done perfectly, if the reign of God prevailed. They are prolepses of what life will be like at that time when God's will reigns in a renewed Earth. What could the miracles of Jesus teach us about God's perfect intention for humans in relationship to creation?

The miracles can be classified as healings, exorcisms, resurrections, and so-called nature miracles in which Christ acted upon nature in some miraculous way. It is particularly in these latter that we might ask what they reveal about Christ's and hence our relationship with the natural world. There are principles of God's will for humans in nature to be discovered in these models.

In the Stilling of the Storm (Matt. 8:23 and parallels), Christ acts on the threat of nature to human welfare. The terror of the disciples reflects the typical response of Hebrews to the sudden storms in the Galilee uplands. Helpless in the face of such a sudden storm, they awaken Jesus. Interestingly, this is the only time Jesus is said to be sleeping in the Gospels. This does not suggest an indifference so much as one who is at peace with the natural world under the will of God. Yet in the face of nature's threat to the disciples, Christ acts in a way to abate the threat of nature. Under His powerful word "there was a great calm" (Matt. 8:26). Jesus acted in a way that contained nature without destroying it. Without being puerile, it might be

183

observed that Jesus did not drain the Sea of Galilee in order to still the storm. He did what was necessary to protect the disciples, but in so doing restored the sea to its ideal condition, a great calm. The sea is now a friend, not an enemy.

As a model for a theology of human-with-nature, this miracle demonstrates several principles. Humans have the right in dominion to tame those natural forces that threaten. Yet at the same time, that taming must be done in a way that does not violate the integrity of the forces and their ideal natural condition. Here is a dominion over nature that does not destroy nature but rather returns nature to its ideal state in communion with the human.

The Feeding of the Five Thousand (Matt. 14:13 and parallels) and the Feeding of the Four Thousand (Matt. 15:32; Mark 8:1) are nature miracles of another sort. Whereas the Stilling of the Storm limited the forces of nature, the feeding miracles enhanced them to meet human need. The Feeding of the Five Thousand is the only miracle recorded in all four Gospels. That is, it made the greatest impact of any miracle. In a world where most of the one hundred million people living around the Mediterranean rim knew hunger, the power to feed riveted attention to Jesus Christ. Within the history of Jesus' own self-consciousness and the nature of His mission, these miracles play a pivotal role. As Mark's account makes clear, the crowd would have made Jesus King. He drove the crowd away and retired to pray. He would not be a bread messiah. But as a subtheme of this, we see Christ using His powers over nature to meet basic human need. In the hands of Christ, the catch of the sea and the produce of the field are so touched as to meet the needs of the maximum number of people.

Without being banal, we should note that Christ did not pollute the sea or threaten animals with insecticides to accomplish His purpose. In His hands, He cared for the maximum number of human needs in a way that did not destroy but rather multiplied. It was a stewardship of opportunity that maximized the moment to meet human need. There is, of course, a considerable difference in human need and human want. We could imply from this that Christian stewards can, under the sovereignty of God, meet human needs without destroying the environment, but cannot meet every human desire in a society of rampant consumerism. A list of American wants across a twenty-four-hour period demonstrates the demands of a consuming society. According to Tom Parker, author of *In One Day: The Things Americans Do*, in one day Americans eat:

> 250,000 pounds of lobster, four million pounds of bacon, 170 million eggs, 12 million chickens, 1.2 million bushels of potatoes, 11,465 licorice twists, 95 tons of sardines, 6.5 million gallons of popcorn, 400,000 gallons of canned corn, 90,000 bushels of fresh carrots, 1.7 million pounds of cheese, 19 million gallons of milk, 1.5 million pounds of lard and 23 million gallons of soft drinks.
>
> They distribute their remaining wealth to the tune of $40 million for prostitution, $12,000 on dental floss, $700 million on entertainment and recreation in general, $2.5 million on washing their cars, $40 million on automobile repairs, $200 million on advertising, $14.3 million on lottery tickets, and $165 million on charity.[9]

These striking statistics demonstrate the rampant consumption of resources by a society bent toward consumption as a natural right. It should go without saying that such moneys as those spent on licorice, soft drinks, lard, and prostitution do not meet human needs but rather human wants. People can live without candy and sex; they do throughout the planet. The mastery of the Lord Jesus over nature in the Feeding of the Five Thousand was to meet human need, not human want. In a model of civilization where human need is met rather than human covetousness, the relationship to the environment would be different. No one can read the above list of American consumption in one day and feel comfortable with that lifestyle as a reflection of biblical stewardship.

One of the most beloved critics of American consumerism was Henry David Thoreau (1817–1862). In his *Walden*, he contrasted his simple life living on the shore of Walden Pond with the complexity of life in Concord:

> Most men, even in this comparatively free country, through mere ignorance and mistake, are so occupied with the factitious cares and superfluously coarse labors of life that its finer fruits cannot be plucked by them. Their fingers, from excessive toil, are too clumsy and tremble too much for that. Actually, the laboring man has not leisure for a true integrity day by day; he cannot afford to sustain the manliest relations to men; his labor would be depreciated in the market. He has no time to be anything but a machine...[10]

In this famous essay Thoreau goes on to describe the empty lives of those driven by the desire to have more. They become slaves of their farms and shops and are digging their own graves. He presented in the essay an alternative to this complexity. Thoreau preserves the individualism of a rugged soul within a solitude of communion with nature and freedom from the complexity of covetousness. This American literary icon reminds us of the vast difference between need and want. Jesus demonstrated in His life and work the difference between meeting the two.

In the Miracle of Walking on the Sea (Matt. 14:25; Mark 6:48) we see another dimension of the stewardship of dominion over nature. The disciples were once again in a sudden storm on the Sea of Galilee. In the fourth watch (3:00 to 6:00 A.M.) Jesus

came to the disciples walking on the water. The very disturbance of nature became the vehicle by which He came to them.
Had there been no storm and no disturbed sea, there would
have been no such approach by the Lord Jesus. Here the threat
of the natural world confirms their own humanity and becomes
the vehicle by which Jesus comes to them. He is Christ both
within and above nature. His stewardship of the natural world
involved both dimensions. When He comes to the boat, He
invites Peter to walk on the water. This is truly an invitation for
people of faith to share his master over nature as threat. When
Peter became more aware of the natural disturbance around
him than of the Christ before him, he began to sink. Peter's
misunderstanding of nature and Christ's power in nature threatens Peter. When they get back to the boat, the wind ceases.

Here we see Christ acting within and above nature for the
preservation of His own people. We should note that the threat-
ening aspect of nature is that which brought Christ to His people. Nature sets the boundaries for human power. It reminds us of
the need for one above nature who can tame nature and rescue
us from our own boundedness within nature. Here we see a stewardship of power over nature. It should serve the ends of reduc-
ing human fear and increasing human faith. It does not destroy
nature, but finds in it an avenue to bring God. Christian stewards
must make that same use of nature today. We should not exploit
nature, but we might have that same dominion over the natural
world to use it as a way of the coming of the Christ. Christ cannot come to His Church today in the exploitation of the natural
world. His desire is to end the tyranny of everything that causes
fear and enslaves the human spirit. This He can do without the
exploitation or destruction of the human environment.

In the Miracle of Turning the Water into Wine (John 2:1), Jesus demonstrates stewardship over nature that meets a different kind of human need. Jesus and His disciples had gone to the wedding at Cana. The wedding wine ran low, a shame to the family. It might have been that the very presence of Jesus and His disciples as extra guests had created the crisis. Jesus commanded that the host go back to the well and draw out water. From the source of the water in the well wine was drawn out (as Westcott and others have noted). Jesus touched the water in the Earth at its wellsprings and created through it wedding wine. This miracle was a sign, that is, it pointed beyond itself to the power of Christ in all of life. He used His power over nature to prevent social embarrassment and meet a real human need in a concrete situation. He was able to touch nature at its source and radically transform it into meeting the needs of the moment and at the same time creating a sign that pointed toward His own lordship. His stewardship of the situation involved a positive use of nature to meet need without an abuse of nature.

In the Catch of Fish (Luke 5:4) and the Second Catch of Fish (John 21:1) we find an interaction between Jesus and humans engaged in supporting themselves from the resources of nature in the Sea of Galilee. He gave them His counsel on where and how to catch fish. In conjunction with His stewardship of the moment, they caught an enormous amount of fish, enough to make both boats begin to sink. Under the sovereignty of Christ, nature will yield enough and more than enough to support human need. Again we see Jesus involved in dominion over nature in a way that does not destroy or disrupt nature. He accelerates those processes already available in the natural world for His purposes, but does not destroy that world in so doing.

The most difficult of Jesus' nature miracles are those two miracles in which He acted destructively of natural life. In the Demons Entering a Herd of Swine (Matt. 8:28 and parallels), Jesus performed an exorcism that resulted in the drowning of a herd of swine. There have been many apologies made for this act that fall short of the mark. For example, it has been said that the herdsmen were Jews and had no business keeping swine to begin with, etc. Such fatuous explanations give us no real understanding of this intriguing story. We should rather understand that human rebellion against God has not only disrupted human wholeness but has also unleashed demonic forces or irrationality that we cannot understand. To rebel against God is to create dark, mysterious forces that effect not only us but the natural world around us. It is the Curse of Eden. Our own profound spiritual disruption disrupts the environment around us. When we are not whole, we unleash demonic forces in the environment that, beyond all rationality, destroy and pollute. The very irrationality of the demonic leaving the demoniac and entering pigs to their own destruction is a metaphor for the rape of the Earth by unthinking demonic forces.

On the other hand, the Withering of the Fig Tree (Matt. 21:18) shows in this acted parable how the coming short of the spiritual world can in some way be illustrated in the coming short of the physical. The disruption in the physical world both reacts to and mirrors the fruitlessness of our own lives in the spiritual dimension.

What do the miracles of Jesus teach us about being-with-nature after the model of Jesus who had dominion and was also a servant? Jesus teaches us that we can use nature for human need without destroying nature in the use of it. The natural world provides enough for human need, but not so much as to meet human covetousness. Nature can become the very vehicle that brings Christ to us. As we struggle under the Curse of Eden to live in the face of hostile nature, Christ is the one for us. Through Him we realize that dark and demonic forces have been unleashed into nature through our own disobedience to our vocation as stewards. Human wholeness sometimes takes place against the tragic backdrop of natural destruction by the furies unleashed in human disobedience. This Christological model of being-with-nature sets the backdrop for a more specific approach to our relationship with the world around us as biblical stewards.

A BIBLICAL THEOLOGY OF ECOLOGY

Smith indicates four imperatives that demand a biblical or theological response to the current ecological crisis, a restatement of stewardship toward the planet.[11] First, Christians must affirm that there is a crisis. As responsible stewards we cannot detach ourselves from that reality. Christians must then respond to the charge that Christianity is a major cause for the current crisis. Such critics as Ian MacHard and Lynn White have charged Christians with being the major cause of exploitation of the environment because of the biblical emphasis on dominion of humans over the world. Next, Christians must respond to the charge of a dualism between spiritual and physical which has discounted the Christian responsibility for the environment. Critics of Christianity have pointed to the Second Coming as an impediment to Christian engagement with this world as it is.

Most seriously is the indictment of monotheism as the root of environmental abuse. Toynbee considers that the entire concept of "subdue" the Earth is "immoral, impractical, and disastrous." Instead, he commends a return to an oriental religious pantheism which might salvage the world for humanity.[12] For Christians this is a ridiculous insult, ignorant both of history and Western civilization. As noted before, if an oriental religious philosophy were environmentally friendly, one would certainly see this in the Orient where the philosophy is indigenous. What Toynbee and others do not recognize is the inherent contradiction in their statements. It is precisely in America, heir of the Western tradition of Judeo-Christian education, that concern for the environment has been the most pronounced. It has not been pronounced because of the absence of that tradition, but because of its presence. If Hinduism and Buddhism are the religious salvation of the environment, India and China do not demonstrate it. The greatest sensitivity in the world to environmental issues has taken place in the United States, where the majority of citizens claim adherence to the Judeo-Christian tradition.

In light of these challenges to the Christian tradition, what shall be the answer?

God is the Creator and Sustainer of the Universe. The universe is not its own explanation. Unlike the belief of some Hindus, the Earth has not existed forever. Behind the big bang theory rests Gen. 1:1. This view has been confirmed by humanity's universal religious consciousness. Humans know a creative impulse in moral and religious experience. This impulse must have an origin. Further, God is pursuing a redemptive purpose in the world. If God is redeeming the world, God must have a place as its Creator. If the Earth is not the creation of God, the only other alternative is an impersonal force that brought the planet into existence. The only two kinds of forces known are personal will and impersonal force.[13] Physical force only forwards what exists. There is not evidence in science that physical force creates from nothing. Only personal will is creative.

God not only creates the world, God preserves the world (Col. 1:17f). There could be no continuation of life in the world without the preserving presence and power of God. God did not wind it up like a clock and walk away. God is both immanent in and separate from God's own creation.

God considers creation in all of its parts to be significant and of value apart from the human. "The Earth is the Lord's, and all its fullness" (Ps. 24:1). In Job 38-41 the astonishing variety of creation is celebrated by God, who in turn addresses the presumptuous arrogance of humans. Humans are to keep the Sabbath so that "your ox and your donkey may rest" (Exod. 23:12). The Sabbath year and the year of jubilee demonstrate God's concern for the land that it be renewed (Lev. 25:1-12). Remarkably, wars against other humans must not devolve into war against nature: "When you besiege a city for a long time, while making war against it in order to take it, you shall not destroy its trees by wielding an ax against them" (Deut. 20:19).

Psalm 104 is a remarkable recitation of God's creation for and care of nature in the particular. God has created the waters, mountains, valleys, springs, beasts, wild donkeys, birds, grass, vegetation, wine, oil, bread, trees, goats, rock badgers, moon, sun, darkness, lions, leviathan, and all else. In Psalm 104, the psalmist not only exults in the Creation, but makes an eloquent statement of its interconnectedness. The springs flow from this hill giving drink to the beasts. Beside this spring the birds nest in the vegetation supported thereby. The Psalm is not only a celebration of creation, but a recognition of its interdependence.

Although God alone is the owner, God allows human use of creation. Productivity in the world stems from God, who gives to humans the ability to create wealth (Deut. 8:1-18). God intends humans to find within the created order that which sustains their needs (Gen. 1:29; 9:2-3). The creation shows God's provision for humanity's needs (Ps. 8:1-9).

God delegates dominion to humans. The *imago dei* as dominion is not a gift imparted without accountability. The dominion of humans over God's creation is a continuing interaction with the will of God for that creation. Humankind is not an autonomous, independent representative of God. Their dominion is in keeping with God's personal intention for creation. Adam and Eve are to protect the Garden (Gen. 2:15). Their maintenance is one of cooperation, not exploitation. The consequence for the misuse of the land is elegantly stated in Job 31:38-40:

> If my land cries out against me,
> And its furrows weep together;
> If I have eaten its fruit without money,
> Or caused its owner to lose their lives;
> Then let thistles grow instead of wheat,
> And weeds instead of barley.

Here there is an explicit statement that exploitation leads to judgment. That human sin reduces the fruitfulness of the Earth is a sustained teaching of the Old Testament. Isa. 24:1-23 presents a stark picture of God's judgment on a planet of rebels. The Earth mourns, the curse devours it and nature becomes sterile. The vine will fail to render the grape, confusion will overtake the cities, the Earth splits open and shakes. Every kind of ecological disaster shakes a planet gone amuck with disobedience toward God. Humanity's relationship with God vitally affects the relationship with nature.

God expects a radical sharing of creation. The Christian work ethic finds a basic motivation in providing for the needs of others. Christians are to work with their hands in order to "have something to give him who has need" (Eph. 4:28). The earliest Christian community at Pentecost in Jerusalem was a model of sharing (Acts 2 and 4). Although some of the circumstances of that community cannot be repeated, nevertheless there is a principle of care within the family of faith that abides. The selling of possessions and the sharing among the needy of the congregation calls for a similar use of stewardship in any generation and situation of the Christian church. The early church existed in a *koinonia* which elemented need on the part of all members. Those who had the means brought those means to the church, which in turn distributed the means to those who had need (Acts 4:34-35). It is recognized that the Pentecostal existence of the church in Jerusalem called for unusual generosity on the part of those Diaspora Jews caught off guard far from home and suddenly converted to Christianity. Yet the principle of a church of radical sharing exists to this day. 1 Tim. 6:6-10 provides a matrix of concern for the church today. Those who are wealthy should be content with that which they have in order to share with those who have less.

Recognize that God takes creation so seriously that God intends to renew creation through cosmic redemption. The saving of souls does not exhaust the intention of the gospel. In contrast to a timeless cycle of oriental pantheistic mysticism, Christianity presents a God who works in time and history toward a goal, the renovation of the cosmos. That goal will be realized in Christ, who is the Creator, Sustainer, and Goal of creation (Col. 1:15-20). The program of cosmic Redemption will be realized in

Christ (Rom. 8:18-30). There will be a new heaven and a new Earth as the result of His intervention in history (2 Pet. 3:10-13). In the face of human repentance God will restore fertility to the land (Ps. 72; Isa. 43:19-21; 55:12-13). The purposes of God for a renewed creation will not ultimately be thwarted. God will prevail in God's original Edenic intention for the Earth.

The biblical epic of Redemption does not end with a timeless, spiritual, disembodied existence. The *telos* of the *eschaton* is a new heaven and a new Earth. Within that new Earth, John sees the New Jerusalem coming down out of heaven (Rev. 21:1-2). The ultimate intention of God is not a spiritual absorption of souls without self. It is the redemption of humans within their own environment. Redeemed humans in a resurrected body suitable for the expression of spiritual life will live in a renewed Earth adapted to that new life.

This expectation was enshrined in the early church view of chiliasm, a belief in the millennium as a reign of Christ. Whatever one might think of this view today, it does emphasize the biblical viewpoint of a redeemed humanity in a redeemed environment. Ancient chiliasm was temporally, intellectually, and geographically diffused. It spans the time from Papias of Hierapolis to Augustine of Hippo Regius. Geographically, it embraces Asia Minor, Egypt, Africa, Rome, and Gaul. Such church fathers as Papias, Justin, Irenaeus, Victorinus of Petau, Lactantius, Commodianus, and Tertullian were all advocates of chiliasm. In the twentieth century, chiliasm or millennialism took a back seat to post-millennialism in the optimism of the early century and amillennialism in the midst of the century as a reaction to the crudities of some millennial materialism. Toward the close of the century it has enjoyed something of a renaissance among evangelical thinkers in the school of "historical millennialism." This school emphasizes the broad idea that humans will be saved in their environment under the reign of Christ, without a specific program or plan as the older dispensational millennialism was disposed to do.

Any stewardship of nature should take seriously that the early church took seriously that humans would be redeemed in their environment wherein God through Christ would reign. What God shall ultimately redeem we must care for now.

THE PRACTICAL CHRISTIAN RESPONSE

In some ways 1988 marked a turning point in Christian attention to the environmental crisis. *The Wall Street Journal* proclaimed 1988 "the year the Earth screamed." Drought, heat, the Yellowstone fires, medical waste pollution, acid rain, ozone depletion, and other crises so dominated the news that *Time* named Earth "Planet of the Year." According to Calvin DeWitt, a leader in Christian environmentalist concerns and director of the Au Sable Institute of Environmental Studies in Michigan, Christians began in unprecedented numbers to hear the Earth groan (Rom. 8:22).[14] Beginning in 1988, masses of Christians began to feel a sense of stewardship for the environment. The trend found enlargement as DeWitt was asked repeatedly to speak on radio talk shows about Christians and the environment. A decade before this time, a Christian with interest in the environment would have had to join the Sierra Club and stop trying to integrate faith and environmental renewal. According to DeWitt, when Christians read the Bible with "ecological eyeglasses" they can find that the entire Kingdom of God leaps off the pages in environmental terms. In an August 1989 gathering at the Au Sable Institute, Ronald Manaham of Grace Seminary stated: "The work of the Last Adam, Christ, must be seen to be as broad as the reach of the damage of the First Adam. The work of Christ impacts all human relationships: those with God, with others, and with creation. If the calling of the Christian is to live out salvation, then one must be about stewardship."[15] Loren Wilkinson of Regent College stated that salvation through Christ is more than a merely personal transaction: "The reconciliation between persons and their Creator is incomplete if it does not include a reconciliation with the creation from which they were estranged."[16] Granted this theological nexus, what are some practical steps being taken by individuals and churches to address the crisis?

Philip N. Joranson and Ken Butigan suggest several practical options for Christians who wish to engage with environmental concerns.[17] The Christian should practice explicit and intentional prayer with reference to the environment. Such prayer should open us to the larger context of our existence on the planet. We should cultivate the love of people which in turn leads to a love for the environment in which people live. We should become thoroughly acquainted with a particular place in the cosmos, a microcosm of creation. Within that place we should learn the ecology. By learning to live with stewardship in one place, we can expand our interest to many places. Individual Christians and congregations should be exposed to rocks, animals, and plants as a cause for the worship of God and God's creation.

Beyond such a prayerful basis, Christians should engage in specific activities which engender an ecological consciousness. Many Christians practice recycling, energy conservation programs, and simple lifestyles. Christians should be familiar with and engaged personally with one area of environmental trouble in their own areas. Christians should join and be actively involved in organizations working on environmental issues. They should promote consciousness of creation in worship and the arts. Christians should practice the enjoyment of nature for itself in a reconnection with the natural world.

The simple keeping of a garden might be one of the best avenues into an awareness of the environment. The world began in a garden. The decision for redemption was made in the Garden of Gesthemane. The world will one day end in a garden by a river in a renewed creation (Revelation 21-22). Eating vegetables from our own garden reminds us that food does not come from grocery stores; it just grows in soil that is part of a larger ecosystem. The composting of vegetable wastes, the nature of photosynthesis, and the tactile experience of actually touching the soil itself all belong to a personal commitment to ecology. Since a garden is in the beginning, middle, and end of sacred history, it would not be a bad place to learn the dimensions of environmental stewardship.

———◦○◦◦○———

Chapter Eight

Directions in Contemporary Stewardship

T he foregoing theological dis-
cussion lays the groundwork for examining some issues in contemporary stewardship. Each of the issues discussed in this
chapter has been the object of entire volumes and copious peri-
odical literature. There have been two unavoidable limitations
to this study. First, it does not exhaust the number of issues in
stewardship today. That would be beyond the scope of any general survey. Further, it does not give an exhaustive treatment of
the subjects discussed. Each would be worthy of a monograph of
examination. This chapter does suggest some directions in the
contemporary stewardship discussion.

STEWARDSHIP OF THE ECONOMY

Generally, believers have considered stewardship a matter of
their personal economy. Yet today many consider stewardship a
concern of economic structures. Prentis L. Pemberton and
Daniel Rush Finn are among those addressing these questions.[1]
Compared with most nations, the United States is still wealthy.
Although many Americans consider that we are "Number

One," we are in fact fourteenth on the list of nations when wealth is measured per capita. Nevertheless, the United States is a wealthy nation.

We consider a person an economic success if that person finds basic satisfaction in employment, enjoys a decent standard of living, has some fringe benefits, is reasonably confident of future benefits, advances, and promotions, and is valued by his or her employer. By that definition forty-six million Americans do not have career employment and are locked into menial jobs or joblessness.

That Jesus Christ intended his church to be concerned for the poor and the distressed rests beyond question. How Christians do that in a pluralistic society where even Christians do not agree on the economy is even more complicated. Christians include those who believe in absolute free enterprise and those who believe in a managed economy for the benefit of the distressed. Christians include those who would abolish all welfare programs and those who hold that the Bible demands welfare programs. There is virtually no issue of social justice on which all believers agree. What then can be done?

A Christian of any economic conviction can make a difference by learning that we do not change social and economic structures alone. Pemberton and Finn call for action through a small disciplined community. It is a community because it consists of a number of independent individuals who covenant together to live a life of economic stewardship based on the Kingdom of God. It is small because it will usually have no more than fifteen or twenty members. It will probably be a subgroup of a congregation. Such a group of concern would meet regularly to be informed of issues and to visit local institutions acting in a redemptive way through the economy: soup kitchens, rescue missions, shelters, etc. The group discusses both local discoveries and reading reports on national issues. Such a group can represent any one of many viewpoints on how to live out the life of Jesus in the community.

Next, such a group can make a covenant to monitor its own consumption. Jesus presented two kinds of followers: foregoers and stewards. The foregoers are those who literally forego a material life to follow Him. Missionaries and other Christian workers can belong to those groups. They literally forego a material lifestyle in order to serve. Most of us, however, are stewards. We enjoy the advantages of a reasonable prosperity, but do so as stewards of consumption. There are three reasons to monitor our own consumption.

- First, the New Testament clearly teaches that a life dominated by the material will be dulled to spiritual values.
- Second, most people in the world live in poverty.
- Third, we should retain a margin to support those who are foregoers.

For American Christians to consume without consciousness of this belies the nature of the gospel. Most significantly, by resisting consumption Christians will have a portion of their income remaining to use in the pursuit of Christian concern. Christians might divide their funds into "use" and "surplus" funds. Use funds are those targeted at our own basic physical and cultural needs. Surplus funds are those to be used in Christian stewardship of giving.

Such a small group of concerned Christians can then wish to work within its own local congregation. This is by no means a holier-than-thou group of agitation. Rather, a small group can lovingly and tenderly assist the larger congregation to move toward more concerns of Jesus in the local setting. This can also be done by networking with other Christians in the area. There are few metropolitan areas without numerous Christians seeking to live Christian lives in terms of the local culture and economy. Such concern must then be acted out. One church in a metropolitan area decided to address hunger in the city. This resulted in a ministry which started a hunger committee, a food pantry, a hospital ministry for homeless people, a church garden project, and other such efforts.

In days of enormous economic upheaval, it is impossible to write a sentence with which everyone, even a majority, would agree. But who can disagree that Christians must be active individually and in small groups to see that God's will is done in public policy and the economy? We cannot adopt the position that our nation is simply too pluralistic for Christians to do anything. Stackhouse observes:

> When pluralism becomes an idol invoked to defend a universal normlessness, it becomes positively perverse. If we worship at the altar of anomie, claiming that everything anybody believes is so subjective that we can say nothing about anything with security, there is no reason even to take God seriously. If everything is so completely "perspectival" that we cannot imagine anything to be true or just or right or good in itself, we face the same problem that Heraclitus faced long ago when he argued that everything is in such a state of flux that we can never step into the same river twice. Yet he wanted to claim that the *fluxus quo* was eternally true and more valid than any other perspective. He did not quite recognize what Einstein seems to have recognized in the twentieth century: that even dealing with relativity demands acknowledgment that reality in flux has constant and pervasive patterns of coherence rooted in stable, transcendent reality. "I shall never believe," he said, "that God plays dice with the world."[2]

In the face of complicated economic questions in the nation, Christians might freeze and claim that everything is relative. This normless existence cannot be the position of Christian stewards. Nor can they simply leave it up to the government as if Christians had no corporate responsibility in a nation of need. It is still relevant to ask the age-old question of the national economy: "What would Jesus do?"

THE STEWARDSHIP OF PEACE

As difficult as a Christian economic stewardship can be in the contemporary world, of equal or similar difficulty is a Christian stewardship of peace. In 1988 the 200th General Assembly of the Presbyterian Church (U.S.A.) and churches of the World Alliance of Reformed Churches were challenged with a report titled, "The Church in Global Society."[3] This wide-reaching report called upon members to be faithful to Jesus Christ and the biblical vision of peace and justice, as well as to work for its manifestation in every possible way. It further called Christians to work through established structures to bring about peace and justice. It even cited John Calvin and John Knox regarding challenging civil authority when unjust structures stand in the way of peace. While some devout believers are uncomfortable with the latter, it is agreed by most Christians that the church should seek peace in the world.

The Bible teaches that God is a God of peace and seeks peace in the world.[4] The great biblical words for peace imply the kind of peace that God seeks. The Hebrews longed for šālôm that was not merely the absence of war but a life of fullness in every positive sense. The Old Testament begins with humans in such a state with God. The Greek word for peace irene speaks not only of the absence of conflict but a right state of mind that comes from reconciliation with God through the Lord Jesus Christ. Jesus called on His followers to follow Him as peacemakers (Matt. 5:9). This means more than stopping war. It creates positive initiatives for peace by taking proactive stances for peace.

From 1496 BC to AD 1861 there were 3,130 years of war and 277 years of peace. The Old Testament followed a policy of Holy War against the enemies of Yahweh. On the other hand, for the first two hundred years of Christian history, Christians were largely pacifists. Most Christians today have accepted the middle view, that of a just war. A just war must have a reasonable chance for success, be for a just cause, be a last resort, fought under legitimate authority, using just means, with a cost proportional to the goal intended, just in its intent, and the intention to conduct war should be announced. By measurement, for example, most Christians believe that the Allied involvement in World War II was justified.

At least from the time of Augustine's letter to Count Boniface in AD 418, Christians have believed it possible to "please God while engaged in military service." During World War II the distinguished theologian Reinhold Niebuhr argued:

> The Christian's role in the specifics of history must compromise Jesus' ideals with the world's necessities. Love, Niehbuhr argued, is an impossible possibility. In the sinfulness of human life, justice is often the best that can be hoped for. The Christian obligation is, therefore, to resist evil, and to keep efforts toward justice under the constant critique of the ideal of love.[5]

The Presbyterian theologian Paul Ramsey argued that pacifism is an unrealistic approach for Christians in a world of such danger as ours. Southern Baptists issued a statement in 1963 called The Baptist Faith and Message. It reads:

> It is the duty of Christians to seek peace with all men on principles of righteousness. In accordance with the spirit and teachings of Christ they should do all in their power to put an end to war.
>
> The true remedy for the war spirit is the gospel of our Lord. The supreme need of the world is the acceptance of His teachings in all the affairs of men and nations, and the practical application of the law of love.[6]

Fortunately, the looming threat of nuclear war has somewhat abated. It is now more possible to consider the reality of limited war. Yet the Christian conscience can never be comfortable with war. Christians should do all they are able to do in every arena of life to make peace. This begins in the personal sphere of influence but must extend to ever-larger areas of concern. Certainly, Christians should be among the first to ask the hard questions of the justice and necessity of any specific war. At the same time Christians must live for justice among humans.

THE STEWARDSHIP OF LEISURE

For many Christians, this form of stewardship can seem as much an oxymoron as "hot ice" or "dry dampness." The American Protestant work ethic has so saturated the perceptions of Christian culture that the bare mention of a stewardship of leisure might seem to be the idea of a theological student or slacker who needed a recondite subject for a thesis.

Yet this is by no means the case. This generation has more leisure on its hands than any in history. A biblical understanding of Christian stewardship with regard to leisure is not only a necessity, but also an urgency. What American Christians do with their leisure time is a question of enormous significance for them and for the culture.

God does not oppose leisure. The creation account announces that God rested following creation. It is obvious that God did not rest out of a sense of exhaustion but out of a sense of completion. God did not have to catch up on sleep in order to have more energy. The divine leisure to complete creation, look at it, and call it very good was part of God's nature. That is, God endorsed God's own leisure for its own sake, not because it rested God to work again. Psalm 135 describes God taking pleasure in that which God has created.

Jesus surely practiced times of leisure in the sense of a retreat from his ordinary activities for refreshment and renewal with God. It was an obvious pattern of His life. At least four times in His ministry He took the Twelve aside for a time of retreat and reflection. He sought time alone for relaxation and reflection. No one could maintain that the life of Jesus Christ was one unabated frantic pace with no stopping. Yet Jesus perfectly did the will of God.

The distinguished theologian J. I. Packer has written cogently on a Christian stewardship of leisure.[7] Packer notes that there is a worldwide trend among Christians to be carried away with consumerism and a market economy. Unless Christians develop a stewardship of leisure, they will be compromised in their ability to act as a counterculture within the larger secular culture. In a world consumed with narcissistic lifestyles, what are the problems in a theology of leisure? Leisure always presents the possibility of idolatry. What controls your life is what you worship. Bob Dylan sang years ago, "You've got to serve somebody." Idols can be anywhere. One can worship a degree, a career, or even one's own employer for whom one will do literally anything. One can idolize work as well as play. Anything can become an addiction. If we do not live for God, to God, and with God, we have lapsed into some kind of idolatry.

There are also problems at both extremes of hedonism and antihedonism. Modern Western culture is largely hedonistic: "If it feels good, do it." It makes a god of the immediate gratification available in the moment. There has more recently been coined a phrase, "Christian hedonism." This ironic phrase catches the sense that God wants God's people to enjoy life in the here and now as well as the there and then. Although this might be an unfortunate choice of words, it does point out that Christians are the most likely to enjoy life in this world today. Christians should also avoid utilitarianism in leisure. This is the attitude that the only value of leisure is to rest one up so one can go back to work. Leisure has no independent value apart from rest in order to work. Says Packer, "So Christians should value leisure as more than a periodic pit stop before further work, and they should resist the narrowing impact of the money- and manufacture-mesmerized mindset that marks utilitarian social thinking."[8]

The Christian does not idolize either work or leisure. Only God deserves worship, not vocation or vacation. Several words speak of the redeemed life. Today the redeemed life is spoken of as "wholeness." Fifty years ago Christians spoke of "balance." Thomas Aquinas spoke of "proportion." Calvin spoke of "moderation." There belongs in the life of the Christian a balance between work and leisure.

Packer suggests several truths that bear on our use and stewardship of leisure:

There is a Duty of Rest. God rested on the seventh day after the six days of creation (Gen. 1:1-2:3). The prescribed flow of

work and rest is part of God's order in creation. God commanded the leisure of a day of worship and rest. We suffer today
from the bleakness in the labor market of demands for a seven-
day week. The harried generation who works at its play is so
tired that it must play at its work.

There is a Goodness in Holy Pleasure. The Bible by no
means limits the rationale for creation to the merely pragmat-
ic. Such biblical works as the Song of Solomon project a love
of beauty, enjoyment of the sensual, and sensitivity to beauty
for beauty's sake.

There is a Joy in Festivity. The Bible is full of feasts. Leviticus
23 records seven holy convocations. Work was prohibited and
celebration was expected on these occasions. At these feasts, as
noted in chapter 2, the Israelites would sometimes share in a
communal meal and festal dining. John 2 records Jesus' presence at the wedding in Cana of Galilee. That Jesus would
attend such an occasion, obviously participate, enjoy it, and
even provide additional wine by a miracle underscores God's
endorsement of celebration, relaxation, and conversation in a
festival atmosphere.

Instructive in this regard is the habit of some highly effective
ministers. Universally regarded as one of the most effective ministers in history is Charles Haddon Spurgeon (d. 1892).
Spurgeon was a prodigious worker with more sermons in print
one hundred years after his death than any preacher in history.
He ran some sixty institutions out of his Metropolitan
Tabernacle in Southwark, London. He believed strongly in rest
for the ministry. His statement was often, "You must unstring the
bow sometimes." He retreated regularly to Mentone on the
French Riviera (before it was the site of jet-setters and glamour).

His life is a remarkable testament to the alternation of very hard work and total leisure. The Rev. R. T. Kendall, D.Phil. oxon, is minister of the world-famous Westminster Chapel in London. He is the successor to G. Campbell Morgan and Martyn Lloyd-Jones. Kendall retires to the Florida Keys for eight weeks each year to do nothing but catch bonefish. He is a masterful pulpiteer and of profound influence in published sermons. Examples such as these could be multiplied.

There is a reality of stewardship in how we spend our leisure time. For most of us that time is limited. Necessity places boundaries on how much time we actually have for leisure. The way we spend that time is a matter of personal stewardship. God intends for people to enjoy the pleasure of leisure. Adam and Eve enjoyed a life of unmitigated pleasure in the Garden. Eden means "garden of pleasure." It has never been God's intention that life be without pleasure. H. L. Mencken defined Puritanism as the haunting fear that somewhere, somehow, somebody might be happy. This was never the intention of God.

There is a difference between happiness and what Jesus called "blessedness," *makaroi*. The blessed life is a life lived beyond the chance of happiness. The Old English word "hap" means "chance." At the very root of mere happiness is a matter of chance. Happiness depends on the external circumstances of life. Because of that it is always subject to the vagaries of human experience in the extreme. The Greeks called Cyprus the *makarios* isle because it contained within its shores everything needed to forge a fulfilling life. It had to import nothing. It exported from its abundance. In the same sense a truly blessed life is free from the need to import resources in order to be happy. It can enjoy the opportunity of leisure not as a frantic weekend search for meaning in life, but the relaxation of a life that already knows fulfillment. Americans find so little fulfillment in leisure, look for ever more recondite and esoteric leisure pursuit, and still face Monday with an emptiness because they do not enter into leisure as people who are at the outset fulfilled in the inward life.

The lack of true recreating leisure today roots in the ignoring of the fourth commandment (Exod. 20:8-11). God ordained that humans should cease from all other pursuits one day per week in order to worship and renew themselves. Even medical science had proved the necessity of that septenary rest period. The failure to observe that commandment devoids leisure of meaning. We do not break the commandments; they break us if we ignore them.

When God's will is honored in life there is the basis for a true leisure that comes not only from the cessation of physical activity but also that rest which comes from spiritual wholeness.

THE STEWARDSHIP OF GENETIC TECHNOLOGY

Developed nations are at the very beginning of a coming onslaught of cultural change brought about by genetic research and manipulation. "Gene speak" might soon replace "psychobabble" as the way people account for their goodness and badness, their triumphs and tragedies.[9] The Human Genome Initiative has become the latter twentieth-century equivalent of the race to the moon in the 1960s. The energies that were once turned outward to discover the lunar surface have now been turned inward to discover the map of the human genetic landscape.

We now face the reality that genetic determinism is becoming an opponent of all traditional anthropologies as an explanation of human behavior. This has moved far beyond heart disease and cancer. Genetic determinism is now involved in psychiatric disorders such as schizophrenia, depression, alcohol, and drug abuse. Even mundane differences in personality, lifestyle, behavior, cognitive development, attitudes, personality, and diet are being ascribed to a genetic determinism. In the face of this, there is the silence of the church toward the claim that human behavior has a component of genetic determinism. Even beyond the speculation about personality and lifestyle, the question is raised by genetic technology as to whether or not the deeper spiritual aspects of humane existence are also the result of genetic codes embedded in the chromosomes of humans. Are such realities as trust, absolute dependence, or the sense of the sacred also genetically determined? To what extent does human DNA contain the encoded message of ancestral adaptive history, adaptive responses that instead of being learned are unconscious and affective because they are part of the genetic inheritance?

The genetic technology further raises questions about the human use of reproductive technology, artificial insemination, in vitro fertilization, genetic engineering, amniocentesis, and other related subjects. Other than the academy where such questions have been studied by theologians and ethicists, the church has been silent in the face of this technological revolution. Darwinism's impact on civilization was speculative. It did not really afford an immediate technological alternative to life. On the other hand, the genetic revolution has raised the possibility of drastic technological change available for the very fabric of existence.

A response of Christian stewardship to this present genetic dilemma is one of the most urgent and demanding responses in contemporary stewardship. Genetic technology will open a world of possibilities heretofore unimagined. To be stewards of genetic technology is to be stewards of a truly godlike power. The ability to predict human behavior of an individual on the basis of genetic makeup,the ability to manipulate genes, and the invasive restructuring of genetic paradigms to achieve socio-political ends are all realities at the door.

A Christian stewardship of this new technology can take one of two views: pessimistic or positive. If genetics are seen only as a reductionistic explanation of human behavior which will result in a Pavlov-style determinism of every aspect of human life and personality, the brave new world of genetic research leads to despair. On the other hand, Lindon Eaves and Lora Gross see within this process a basis for "grace within the structure of life itself." As they put it in rather optimistic language:

> In the mechanisms of inheritance and gene action, through the processes of genetic mutation, recombination, nonadditive interactions between genes, and interactions between new generic constitutions and the ecosystem, we encounter the promise of new lives with the creativity and courage of a Moses, Judith, Jesus, Buddha, Gandhi, Muhammad, Theresa, Biko, or the martyrs of the Third World. Such grace is inherent in nature and offers the fragile promise of its completion by redirecting the resources of the ecosystem into more abundant life . . . Several times in their history, the material processes of life have produced a person who transcends all conventional definitions of personhood to the point where the term freedom is the best we have available. Put crudely, if Jesus, and men and women like him, are "determined," we'll settle for that kind of determinism![10]

In such opinions as that, we see the optimistic side of the genetic theo-philosophical debate. Genetic research is too cutting edge at this point to make any determinations about its long-term implications for human behavior. A stewardship of this technology cannot simply endorse it with the gushing optimism of Eaves and Gross. The willingness to capitulate immediately to the latest scientific journal report of genetic encoding as it relates to human behavior will not mark appropriate stewardship of genetic research.

Questions of freedom and determinism are among the oldest in theology and philosophy. These questions must be brought in all of their historical significance to the emerging disciplines of genetic research. Christians have the stewardship of asking hard questions about the findings of such research:

- Does the deterministic bias of science inform the conclusions of genetic research into human personality?
- The Christian worldview a priori insists on the redemptive use of technology. The church must bring that redemptive perspective to all emerging technologies, i.e., will the use of this technology have the greatest redemptive outcome for the greatest number of people involved.
- The Christian must hold up to scrutiny every indication that humans are absolved of moral responsibility because of genetic predisposition. The wild possibility that no one will be accountable for anything because of deterministic genetic constructs would hold civilization as hostage.
- The use of genetic technology to alter the landscape of life will require the most diligent theological thought ever brought to a modern technological process. There is a givenness in creation which cannot be altered within the bounds of reverent living. The temptation of Eden was to play God. If even scientists stepped back from the power they unleashed in nuclear fusion and fission to declare its

use unthinkable in warfare, they can be called to step back from genetic manipulation for the same purposes.

• Genetic change can be used to enhance life as we know it. Strange, new resistant viruses are appearing throughout the planet, the Ebola virus being an example. As the specter of new plagues haunts the planet, the survival of life as it now is could depend upon the protective devices of genetic manipulation.

The Christian faith confesses that in the Virgin Birth of Jesus Christ, God entered into the human genetic situation. In the miracle of Bethlehem the twenty-four chromosomes of Mary in some way were enhanced by twenty-four chromosomes supplied by divine miracle to produce Jesus Christ. The Virgin Birth implies that God can act in human history at the genetic level. The stewardship of this powerful technology must apply that fact to the emerging genetic technology.

THE STEWARDSHIP OF HEALTH CARE

A matter of urgent concern to every American citizen is the national stewardship of health care. In the last decade this stewardship involved the use of so-called heroic measures to save lives in unusual circumstances. With the current universal presence of HMOs (Health Maintenance Organizations), the stewardship involves the question of who gets minimum treatment.

We live in the era of the patient as customer rather than the patient as the object of mercy. This is the contradiction of a thousand years of Western civilization. The hospital movement in Western civilization began in cathedrals and monasteries where provision was made in hostels for the indigent. They were for the poor and they were free. In the nineteenth century, hospitals began renting rooms to private patients. Because of an efficiency of scale joined to an increasingly effective technology, hospitals became centers of financial power and potential. In the last decade, the debate raged about the level of governmental underwriting for the hospital/medical structure in America. Today the debate has shifted.

The managed care movement of HMOs dominates the industry. Decisions that were once made by physicians are now made by business people, literally down to whether or not a given individual gets a blood test. Recent national scandal has been the response to hospitals requiring new mothers to be out in forty-eight hours, and in some instances twenty-four, after giving birth. Further studies have indicated that doctors are rewarded on the basis of capitation for not treating patients. Doctors claim that they are being told to withhold vital information or even to lie in order to decrease spending on the patient.

The HMO takes in a finite amount of money from corporations. Actual healing ministry to patients becomes a liability, on the loss side of the balance sheet. Everett L. Wilson raises a painful analogy on the basis of the parable of the good Samaritan. In terms of medical care, who is my neighbor? "The Samaritan's example gives us no warrant for treating mercy like a marketable commodity. When there is a choice to be made because of limited resources, the ability of the patient to buy them is irrelevant to Christian ethics."[11] There is a great difference between asking "Who is my neighbor?" and "Who is my customer?" Who is the neighbor in a city where hospitals are no longer outposts of mercy, but are businesses searching not for the sick but for their share of the health care market? The man in the ditch on the road to Jericho was not a customer or a business partner, he was a person in distress in need of immediate attention from those who walked by.

In the HMO system, the salaries of specialists who are more likely to deal with gravely ill people are being slashed in city after city. In some instances, the charges allowed for specialized procedures have been cut to the point that such specialists are leaving managed care altogether, to serve only those who can afford it.

In the United States, it appears that the public has said a resounding "No" to further federal government intrusion into the health care of the nation. This has moved the problem into the hands of private business. In the past, the great hospitals in many cities were those founded by the denominations. Even these are now closing or being secularized to the point that their Christian connection is in name only.

A Christian stewardship response will be demanded for this emerging national crisis of health care. In the face of the profit motive having replaced the mercy motive in health care, Christians must be the prophetic voice for mercy. This does not mean that everybody can have all the health care anybody wants. It does mean that mercy must dominate over business in the Christian stewardship of health. For Christians the question must not be, "Who can pay?" Rather, the question must be, "How do we use the resources we have to serve the most people in the name of Christ?"

Fortunately, as we approach the last days of this century, there does appear to be a slight ray of hope for a more merciful approach to health care. While the national caregivers still make life and death decisions based on the corporate bottom line, there is a developing national trend toward a less mercenary approach. One can only hope the pendulum will once again swing toward the direction of a Christ-like concern for those who find themselves in need of medical services.

THE CHRISTIAN STEWARDSHIP OF DEATH

We so often speak of the stewardship of life that we seldom address the stewardship of death. As is often said, "Heaven is my home, but I'm not homesick yet." For that reason we seldom address the stewardship in life's final passage from this life to the life beyond.

The Bible really indicates more than one kind of death. William Hendricks addressed this in a typically analytical and focused way. He describes the levels of death:

- First, when we are able to respond to God, the self, and others at all levels—biologically, psychosocially, and spiritually—we are fully alive.
- Second, when we are not able to respond to God biologically, psychosocially, or spiritually, we are dead physically, psychosocially, and spiritually.
- Third, when we are unable or unwilling to respond to God spiritually but respond to others and ourselves at the biological and spiritual stages, we are spiritually dead.
- Fourth, when we are unable or unwilling to respond to God, the self, or others psychologically or socially, we are psychosocially dead, as in persons who have withdrawn from reality.[12]

In this regard, we should exercise a stewardship of life and death in each of the areas of biological life, psychosocial life, and spiritual life. To be dead in any of the three areas is to be out of the total stewardship of life.

Yet the Christian faces physical death. The hope of the Christian is the Resurrection of the Lord Jesus Christ and the reality of heaven. The Bible speaks of heaven in metaphorical language. The Tree of Life in the Garden indicates heaven as a place of God's eternal provision for us (Rev. 22:2). The walled city points to God's ultimate protection of us (Rev. 21:11-27). The Tabernacle of God in the midst of the city reminds us of God's presence with us (Rev. 21:3). That presence is one of an intimate family, a closeness with the Son of God whom we love and whom we serve. Heaven will be a place of completion where the loose ends of life will be tied up, unfinished things finished, and unexplained things explained. Heaven will be a corporate society where God's people of the ages will be gathered together forever. All of these realities form the Christian hope as it relates to heaven.

The Christian can face the end of physical life on Earth because of the certainty of eternal resurrection life in heaven. The world-famous Christian ethicist, Dr. T. B. Maston, maintained that the Christian should not fear death. It is indeed the enemy, but for the Christian, death is also the friend. When Jesus broke the chain of death against the marble wall of the sepulchre and emerged victorious, He transformed forever the terror of death.

In light of this the Christian has the opportunity in hope to be a steward of earthly life's final experience. This involves a number of decisions and activities that are wise to make in advance.

The Christian steward of death will want to decide on whether or not to make a living will indicating the desire or lack thereof for heroic measures to be taken to sustain his or her life. These have become so common in the later twentieth century that virtually any church can guide a member into an understanding of the preparation of such an instrument. This enables the Christian person to relieve the family of the burden of the decision of prolonging life when only invasive procedures can prolong life.

The Christian steward will make a will and keep that will updated and stored in a known place. It is an absolute shame for a Christian to die intestate. In Texas, for example, 75 percent of the adult residents do not have a will. If you die without a will, the state has a will for you. The state will divide your inheritance and your family will have nothing to say about it. It is an act of selfishness and carelessness not to have a will. To spend a lifetime of Christian stewardship and then to die without a will is a tragedy. If you cannot afford a lawyer, most office supply stores and bookstores now have a kit to make your own will. It is best to use a probate attorney who can advise you about your own best interests.

For most breadwinners, it is wise to have life insurance. This insurance should be the most inexpensive term insurance bought from a rated life insurance company. A person should have from four to five times his or her annual earnings in a life insurance policy. The average working person cannot save enough to cover the sudden expenses a family faces in the event of unexpected death. The kindest thing to be done for a family is to provide for them in death as in life.

A Christian steward should make prearrangements for final expenses. In the twentieth century, the cost of final expenses has doubled every ten years. The funeral industry has established that people who wait until the crisis of death and who make final decisions at the time of loss spend on the average 60 percent more than those who make decisions in calm deliberation before death. In seven out of ten instances, it will be the death of a husband before that of a wife. In one moment the wife has lost breadwinner, companion, and credit reference. She must go to the cemetery and choose a piece of property for final burial. Then she must go into a funeral home, choose a casket and a funeral service. She must then pay for it on the spot. Funeral homes do not extend credit other than the assignment of life insurance policies for final expenses. Such a widow is making decisions of enormous significance in the immediate aftermath of the greatest loss in her life.

Further, the arrangement of services often becomes a time of family conflict, unless decisions are made in advance. Children in a family might have vastly different expectations of a memorial service. How much heartache is saved when one lets his or her intentions be known years before the crisis so that all is settled.

Most states provide for a simple trust or insurance policy to be bought through a funeral provider. These freeze the costs of final expenses so that they can never escalate. These trust instruments can usually be cashed in or transferred if a family should move. They are normally to be paid for in very low monthly installments affordable to most families. They even provide credit life insurance policies to cover the balance in case death occurs before the trust is funded.

Virtually no families ever say at the time of death that they are sorry their loved one prearranged services. On the other hand, the sad testimony of many families at the time of death is the wish that plans had been made and the burden had been lifted.

In addition to these plans, every Christian steward should keep a file folder including all vital records. Insurance policies, retirement funds, social security records, veteran's records, and the plans for final services should all be in that folder. In that way the survivors will be able to pursue in death the same stewardship of resources that the decedent practiced in life.

THE STEWARDSHIP OF THE GOSPEL

It would hardly be fitting to end a book on stewardship with an emphasis on death rather than life. The Christian is involved in the stewardship of the message of eternal life. No greater stewardship is imaginable than that of the gospel of Jesus Christ. The apostle Paul indicated this trusteeship in 1 Cor. 4:1: "Let a man so consider us, as servants of Christ and stewards of the mysteries of God." Here the apostle combines two magnificent images.

The word "servant" translates the Greek term *hupēretes*. The term is indicative of the galley slave who rowed at the lowest, darkest level of the Roman trireme. There the oars were the longest, the air was the hottest, and the prisoners chained to the oars were the most despised. The mighty apostle in evident humility considered himself as "God's under-rower." It is a striking metaphor to express his personal desire to be the servant of Christ.

Yet in the next pen stroke, Paul elevates the concept to another dimension. He is a steward of the mystery of God. For us today the word "mystery" describes a detective story which one can, if careful attention is given to the clues, puzzle out before the plot finally reveals the denouement. That is not what the word means in the New Testament. The *musterion* is that which God conceals and which humans can only know because God has revealed it. For two thousand years, humanity had waited since the promise to Abraham that God would bless the Earth through him for the revelation of that great mystery. In the Advent of Jesus Christ, God's secret became an open secret.

The greatest stewardship in the world is the stewardship of that open secret that God has come to save humans and humanity through the gospel of Jesus Christ.

God deserves that the world hear that message of God's invasion into history in the person of Jesus Christ. In these days when cultic movements will give a double and even triple tithe to spread a message of error and confusion, how can we refuse to respond with open heart and open hand to that which God would have us give?

A missionary sat beside the Strait of Malaka off the coast of Malaysia near Kuala Lumper. He told a visitor from America story after story of Malaysian Moslems who had lost literally everything to become Christians. Their families disowned them, their bosses fired them, their government destroyed their very identities so that they became nonpeople. Yet they joyously gather on Sunday to celebrate the change that the Lord Jesus has brought into their lives. To contrast this with the reluctance of affluent American Christians to give at a level of stewardship commensurate with their incomes is an astonishment.

One of the greatest pulpiteers in American history was the late Dr. George Truett. So effective and moving was Truett's appeal to give that he saved his own university before he enrolled as a freshman by traveling the towns and cities of Texas appealing for his soon-to-be school. One striking scene stands out from Truett's life:

> While making such a heart-moving appeal to give one's life and then one's substance, the deacons passed around very large wicker baskets. In the back of the sanctuary a little boy, off the streets, an urchin who had nothing to give, asked for the deacon to put the basket on the floor. The little boy got into the basket. He said, "I'll give me." Decades later the people who

witnessed that scene described it as a life-changing moment for everyone present.

Stewardship begins with that commitment: "I'll give me." All else follows as sunrise follows night.

Notes

Chapter 1

1. Walter Eichrodt, "In the Beginning: A Contribution to the Interpretation of the First Word of the Bible," in *Creation in the Old Testament*, ed. Bernhard W. Anderson (Philadelphia: Fortress Press, 1984), p. 72.
2. Gerhard von Rad, *Old Testament Theology*, vol.1, *The Theology of Israel's Historical Traditions*, trans. D. M. G. Stalker (New York: Harper and Bros., 1962), p. 143.
3.   Ibid., p. 139.
4. Robert Butterworth, "The Theology of Creation," in *Theology Today*, gen ed. Edward Yarnold (Notre Dame, Indiana: Fides Publishers, 1969), p. 40.
5. Christoph Barth, *God With Us: A Theological Introduction*, ed. Geoffrey W. Bromiley (Grand Rapids: Eerdmans), p. 21.
6. Douglas John Hall, *The Steward: A Biblical Symbol Come of Age*, rev. ed. (Grand Rapids: Eerdmans), p. 26.
7. Emil Brunner, *Man in Revolt*, trans. Olive Wyon (Philadelphia: The Westminster Press, 1947), p. 83.
8. Samuel R. Driver, *Genesis*, Westminster Commentary, p.15.
9. Karl Barth, *Nein!* quoted in Brunner, Ibid., p. 95.

10. Ibid., pp. 97–98.

Chapter 2

1. Hans Walter Wolff, *Anthropology of the Old Testament*, trans. Margaret Kohl (Philadelphia: Fortress Press, 1974), p. 159.
2. Ibid., p. 160.
3. Ibid., p. 161.
4. Ludwig Kohler, *Der hebraische Mensch* (Tübingen: Mohr, 1953), p. 112.
5. John P. Milton, *God's Covenant of Blessing* (Rock Island, Illinois: Augustana Press, 1961), p. xi.
6. Eliezer Schweid, *The Land of Israel: National Home or Land of Destiny* (Rutherford, New Jersey: Herzl University Press, 1985), pp. 16–20.
7. Andrew Harper, "The Book of Deuteronomy," in *Expositor's Bible* (New York: A. C. Armstrong and Son, 1905), p. 359.
8. Albert C. Knudson, *The Religious Teaching of the Old Testament* (New York: Abingdon-Cokesbury Press, 1918), p. 308.
9. Herman Schultz, *Old Testament Theology*, trans. J. A. Paterson (from the 4th German ed.; Edinburgh: T. & T. Clark, 1892), I, 378.
10. W. O. E. Oesterley, *Sacrifices in Ancient Israel* (New York: The MacMillan Company, n.d.), p. 97.
11. H. H. Rowley, *The Missionary Message of the Old Testament* (London: The Carey Press, n.d.), p. 32.

Chapter 3

1. S. R. Driver, *Deuteronomy*, International Critical Commentary (New York: Charles Scribner's Sons, 1895), p. 172.

2. Henry Lansdell, *The Sacred Tenth* (London: Society for Promoting Christian Knowledge, 1906).
3. Ibid., p. 3.
4. Ibid., p. 7.
5. Ibid., p. 8.
6. Ibid., p. 17.
7. Ibid., pp. 14–15.
8. Ibid., p. 15.
9. Ibid., p. 17.
10. Ibid., p. 22.
11. Ibid., p. 24.
12. Ibid., pp. 24–25.
13. Ibid., p. 26.
14. Ibid., p. 28.
15. Ibid., p. 29.
16. Ibid., p. 30.
17. Ibid., p. 35.
18. Sayce, *Patriarchal Palestine* (London: SPCK, 1895), p.175.

Chapter 4

1. C. E. B. Cranfield, *Romans*, The International Critical Commentary, 2nd series, p. 414.
2. Donald Tuzin, "The Voice of Gods," *Discover* (September 1985):18.
3. George Eldon Ladd, *A Theology of the New Testament* (Grand Rapids: Eerdmans, 1974), p. 482.

Chapter 5

1. Archibald M. Hunter, *The Parables Then and Now* (Philadelphia: The Westminster Press, 1971), p. 118.

2. Ibid., pp. 99–100.

3. Ruth Ann Foster, "Stewardship: Sign and Substance of the Christian Life as Taught in the New Testament," *Southwestern Journal of Theology* 37 (Spring 1995):15.

4. James Stalker, *The Ethic of Jesus* (New York: George E. Doran Co., 1909), p. 323.

5. L. H. Marshall, *The Challenge of New Testament Ethics* (London: Macmillan & Co. Ltd., 1960), p. 137.

Chapter 6

1. Barry Tarshis, *The Average American Book* (New York: Atheneum, 1979), pp. 36, 82.

2. Otto Michel, "Oikonomos," *Theological Dictionary of the New Testament* (Grand Rapids: Eerdmans, 1967), 5:149–151.

3. Helge Brattgard, *God's Stewards*, trans. Gene J. Lund (Minneapolis: Augsburg, 1963): pp. 41–42.

Chapter 7

1. Holmes Rolston, "Rights and Responsibilities on the Home Planet," *Zygon* 28/4 (1993):425.

2. Ibid., p. 425.

3. Ebbie C. Smith, "Environlove: The Christian Approach to Ecology," *Southwestern Journal of Theology* 37 /2 (1950):23-31.

4. William A. Dryness, "Are We Our Planet's Keeper," *Christianity Today* (April 8, 1991):40–42.

5. Bill DeVall and George Sessions, *Deep Ecology: Living as If Nature Mattered* (Salt Lake City: Peregrine Smith Books, 1985), p. 65.

6. James Lovelock, *The New Scientist* 65 (1975):304, quoted in

Peter de Vos et al, *Earth Keeping in the Nineties: Stewardship of Creation* (Grand Rapids: Eerdmans, 1980), p. 196.

7. Fritjof Capra, *The Turning Point: Science, Society and the Rising Culture* (New York: Bantam Books, 1982), pp. 91–92.

8. Douglas John Hall, *Imaging God* (Grand Rapids: Eerdmans, 1986), p. 128.

9. Tom Parker, *In One Day: The Things Americans Do*, published by Houghton Mifflin, quoted in *The Toronto Globe and Mail*, 10 January 1985, and also cited in Hall, *Imaging*, p. 207, note 2.

10. Reginald L. Cook, *Thoreau Society Bulletin*, Winter, 1953, cited in Sculley Bradley et al, *The American Tradition in Literature*, 3rd ed., vol.1 (New York: W. W. Norton & Co., 1967), p. 1243.

11. Smith, "Environlove," p. 25.

12. Arnold Toynbee, "The Religious Background for the Present Ecological Crisis," in *Ecology and Religion in History*, ed. David Spring and Eileen Spring (New York: Harper and Row, 1974), 145–46, cited in Smith, "Environlove," 25.

13. Walter Thomas Conner, *Revelation and God* (Nashville: Broadman Press, 1936), p. 267.

14. Kristi G. Streiffert, "The Earth Groans and Christians are Listening," *Christianity Today* (September 22, 1989):38–40.

15. "Ecology Theology," *Christianity Today* (September 22, 1989):41.

16. Ibid., p. 41.

17. Philip N. Joranson and Ken Butigan, eds., *Cry of the Environment: Rebuilding the Christian Creation Tradition* (Santa Fe, New Mexico: Bear & Co., 1984), pp. 436-438.

Chapter 8

1. Prentis L. Pemberton and Daniel Rush Finn, *Toward a Christian Economic Ethic* (Minneapolis: Winston Press, 1985), pp.1–25.
2. Max L. Stackhouse, *Public Theology and Political Economy* (Grand Rapids: Eerdmans, 1987), p. 159.
3. *Church and Society* 78/6, (July/August 1988):8–39.
4. Ronald D. Sisk, "World Peace," in *Understanding Christian Ethics*, ed. William M. Tillman, Jr. (Nashville: Broadman Press, 1988), pp. 203–225.
5. Ibid., p. 217.
6. Ibid., p. 218.
7. J. I. Packer, "Leisure and Life-Style: Leisure, Pleasure, and Treasure," in *God and Culture: Essays in Honor of Carl F. H. Henry*, ed. D. A. Carson and John D. Woodbridge (Grand Rapids: Eerdmans, 1993), pp. 358–68.
8. Ibid., p. 361.
9. Lindon Eaves and Lora Gross, "Exploring the Concept of Spirit as a Model for the God-World Relationship in the Age of Genetics," *Zygon* 27/3 (1992):26–83.
10. Ibid., pp. 274–75
11. Everett L. Wilson, "When Mercy Becomes a Business," *Christianity Today* (February 19, 1990):22–23.
12. William L. Hendricks, *A Theology of Aging* (Nashville: Broadman Press, 1986), pp. 24–25.

Select Bibliography

Books

Barth, Christoph. *A Theological Introduction*. Edited by Geoffrey W. Bromiley. Grand Rapids: Eerdmans.

Brattgard, Helge. *God's Stewards*. Translated by Gene J. Lund. Minneapolis: Augsburg Publishing House, 1963.

Brunner, Emil. *Man in Revolt*. Translated by Olive Wyon. Philadelphia: The Westminster Press, 1947. Barth, Karl. *Nein!* quoted in Brunner.

Butterworth, Robert. "The Theology of Creation" in *Theology Today*. General editor Edward Yarnold. Notre Dame, Indiana: Fides Publishers, 1969.

Capra, Fritjof. *The Turning Point: Science, Society and the Rising Culture*. New York: Bantam Books, 1982.

Conner, Walter Thomas. *Revelation and God*. Nashville: Broadman Press, 1936.

Cook, Reginald L. *Thoreau Society Bulletin*, Winter 1953 in Sculley Bradley et al, *The American Tradition in Literature*. 3rd ed., vol.1. New York: W. W. Norton & Co., 1967.

Cranfield, C. E. B. Romans. *The International Critical Commentary*, 2nd series. Edinburgh: T.T. Clark, 1975–79.

Devall, Bill, and George Sessions. *Deep Ecology: Living as If Nature Mattered*. Salt Lake City: Peregrine Smith Books, 1985.

Driver, Samuel R. *Deuteronomy*. International Critical Commentary. New York: Charles Scribner's Sons, 1895.

_____*Genesis*. Westminster Commentary. London: Methven, 1915.

Eichrodt, Walter. "In the Beginning: A Contribution to the Interpretation of the First Word of the Bible." *Creation in the Old Testament*. Edited by Bernhard W. Anderson. Philadelphia: Fortress Press, 1984.

Hall, Douglas John. *The Steward: A Biblical Symbol Come of Age*. rev. ed. Grand Rapids: Eerdmans, 1982.

_____*Imaging God*. Grand Rapids: Eerdmans, 1986.

Harper, Andrew. *The Book of Deuteronomy* in *Expositor's Bible*. New York: A. C. Armstrong and Son, 1905.

Hendricks, William L. *A Theology of Aging*. Nashville: Broadman Press, 1986.

Hunter, Archibald M. *The Parables Then and Now*. Philadelphia: The Westminster Press, 1971.

Joranson, Philip, and Ken Butigan, editors. *Cry of the Environment: Rebuilding the Christian Creation Tradition*. Santa Fe, New Mexico: Bear & Co., 1984.

Knudson, Albert C. *The Religious Teaching of the Old Testament*. New York: Abingdon-Cokesbury Press, 1918.

Kohler, Ludwig. *Der hebraische Mensch*. Tübingen: Mohr, 1953.

Ladd, George Eldon. *A Theology of the New Testament*. Grand Rapids: Eerdmans, 1974.

Lansdell, Henry. *The Sacred Tenth*. London: Society for Promoting Christian Knowledge, 1906.

Marshall, L. H. *The Challenge of New Testament Ethics*. London: Macmillan & Co. Ltd., 1960.

Milton, John P. *God's Covenant of Blessing*. Rock Island, Illinois: Augustana Press, 1961.

Oesterley, W. O. E. *Sacrifices in Ancient Israel*. New York: The MacMillan Company, n.d.

Packer, J. I. "Leisure and Life-Style: Leisure, Pleasure, and Treasure," in *God and Culture: Essays in Honor of Carl F. H. Henry*. Editors D. A. Carson and John D. Woodbridge. Grand Rapids: Eerdmans, 1993.

Parker, Tom. *In One Day: The Things Americans Do*. Boston: Houghton Mifflin, 1984. As quoted in *The Toronto Globe and Mail*, 10 January 1985, cited in Hall, Imaging, p. 207, note 2.

Pemberton, Prentis L., and Finn Daniel Rush. *Toward a Christian Economic Ethic*. Minneapolis: Winston Press, 1985.

Rowley, H. H. *The Missionary Message of the Old Testament*. London: The Carey Press, n.d.

Sayce, Archibald Henry. *Patriarchal Palestine*. London: The Society for Promoting Christian Knowledge, 1895.

Schultz, Herman. *Old Testament Theology*. Translated by J. A. Paterson (from the 4th German ed.) Edinburgh: T. & T. Clark, 1892.

Schweid, Eliezer. *The Land of Israel: National Home or Land of Destiny*. Rutherford, New Jersey: Herzl University Press, 1985.

Sisk, Ronald D. "World Peace," in *Understanding Christian Ethics*. Editor William M. Tillman, Jr. Nashville: Broadman Press, 1988.

Stackhouse, Max L. *Public Theology and Political Economy*. Grand Rapids: Eerdmans, 1987.

Stalker, James. *The Ethic of Jesus*. New York: George E. Doran Co., 1909.

Tarshis, Barry. *The Average American Book*. New York: Atheneum, 1979.

Toynbee, Arnold. "The Religious Background for the Present Ecological Crisis," in *Ecology and Religion in History*. Editors David Spring and Eileen Spring. New York: Harper and Row, 1974.

von Rad, Gerhard. *Old Testament Theology. Vol. 1, The Theology of Israel's Historical Traditions*. Translated by D. M. G. Stalker. New York: Harper and Bros., 1962.

Wolff, Hans Walter. *Anthropology of the Old Testament*. Translated by Margaret Kohl, Philadelphia: Fortress Press, 1974.

Periodicals and Articles

Dryness, William. "Are We Our Planet's Keeper." *Christianity Today* (April 8, 1991).

Eaves, Lindon, and Lora Gross. "Exploring the Concept of Spirit as a Model for the God-World Relationship in the Age of Genetics." *Zygon* vol. 27, no. 3 (September 1992).

Foster, Ruth Ann. "Stewardship: Sign and Substance of the Christian Life as Taught in the New Testament." *Southwestern Journal of Theology* 37 (Spring 1995).

Lovelock, James. *The New Scientist* 65 (1975). See also 304 in Peter de Vos et al *Earth Keeping in the Nineties: Stewardship of Creation*.Grand Rapids: Eerdmans, 1980.

Rolston, Holmes. "Rights and Responsibilities on the Home Planet." *Zygon* 28/4 (December 1993).

Smith, Ebbie C. "Environlove: The Christian Approach to

Ecology." *Southwestern Journal of Theology* 37/2 (Spring 1950).

Streiffert, Kristi. "The Earth Groans and Christians are Listening." *Christianity Today* (September 22, 1989).

Tuzin, Donald Tuzin, "The Voice of Gods." *Discover* (September 1985).

Wilson, Everett L. "When Mercy Becomes a Business." *Christianity Today* (February 19, 1990).

Index of Subjects

Index of Ancient and Modern Authors

Index of Scripture Citations

Index of Hebrew and Greek Terms